AF698064

# STATE-LOCAL FINANCES IN THE LAST HALF OF THE 1970s

WITHDRAWN

HJ
275
S72

A10202 478072

# STATE-LOCAL FINANCES IN THE LAST HALF OF THE 1970s

David J. Ott • Attiat F. Ott
James A. Maxwell • J. Richard Aronson

American Enterprise Institute for Public Policy Research
Washington, D. C.

This is the fourth study to result from the AEI Long Range Budget Projection Project. Contributors to this volume are DAVID J. OTT, professor of economics at Clark University, ATTIAT F. OTT, professor of economics at Clark University, JAMES A. MAXWELL, emeritus professor of economics at Clark University, and J. RICHARD ARONSON, professor of economics at Lehigh University. This study was made under the overall direction of DAVID J. OTT.

DAVID J. OTT and ATTIAT F. OTT are adjunct scholars of the American Enterprise Institute.

ISBN 0-8447-3157-9

Domestic Affairs Study 29, April 1975

Library of Congress Catalog Card No. 75-7802

© 1975 by American Enterprise Institute for Public Policy Research, Washington, D. C. Permission to quote from or to reproduce materials in this publication is granted when due acknowledgment is made.

*Printed in the United States of America*

# CONTENTS

# SUMMARY OF FINDINGS

The budget of the state and local government sector of the American economy can be broken into two parts: the general government account and the receipts and expenditures of state and local trust funds. Through 1969 the state and local sector was generally characterized by deficits of increasing size on the general government account offset by surpluses of increasing size in the trust fund accounts, with the deficits and surpluses just about offsetting each other. In the period from 1970 to 1972, however, the pattern changed: the general government account deficit grew smaller in 1970 and 1971, became a surplus in 1972, and was roughly in balance in 1973; and the trust fund surplus continued to grow (though only slightly in 1973). As a result, the state and local government sector showed large surpluses during the period, particularly in 1972.

This study finds a strong likelihood of a continued trend toward large and growing surpluses for the state and local sector as a whole in a full employment setting. Depending on the inflation assumption, the combined surplus should be around \$15 billion to \$17 billion in 1980. While the 1970–1973 change in the general government account may have been mostly a temporary phenomenon, there are nevertheless long-run forces which should produce permanent (albeit less spectacular) change in the same direction in the last half of the seventies. In particular, the decline in the birth rate (and therefore in the number of school children and in school construction) together with expected growth in federal grants for construction of antipollution facilities should improve the general government budget picture.

The projected balance in the general government account (assuming zero to 4 percent inflation) ranges from −\$4.1 billion to \$1.4 billion in 1976 to −\$2.2 billion to \$1.6 billion in 1980. There is thus a projected gradual improvement in the general government budget balance with either inflation assumption, as contrasted with the trend toward larger deficits in the 1950s and 1960s. This may be translated into lower pressure for tax rate increases than has been experienced in the past two decades. It has been estimated that the projected expenditures on the general government account (national income accounts basis) could be financed with no increase in tax rates for the sector as a whole (although some states or municipalities may of course require increases and others may be able to cut taxes).

Projected surpluses for the state and local trust funds turn out to be sensitive, in the short run, to the inflation assumption (that is, a higher rate of inflation increases the trust fund surplus). For zero to 4 percent inflation, trust fund surpluses should be between $7 billion and $10 billion in 1976 and between $15 billion and $18 billion for 1980. The trust fund projection model assumes that state and local pension plans continue the average degree of funding holding true for the 1972–1973 data. It is of course difficult to predict to what degree state and local units will fund their pension plans in the future, but the estimates made here provide a benchmark for projections.

When governmental contributions to the trust funds are included as an expenditure to be financed, the outlook for increases in state and local tax rates depends largely on the rate of inflation. At inflation rates below 4 percent it seems likely that, overall, the state and local sector should be able to finance its expenditures (including governmental contributions to the trust funds) with little or no tax increase. In any case, the pressure for tax increases should, for the sector as a whole, be less than in the 1950s and 1960s.

# 1
# INTRODUCTION

Before 1972, economists making forecasts paid relatively little attention to the state and local government sector of the economy. Most of their attention was concentrated on the federal budget and the actions of the Federal Reserve. While the state and local sector had grown at an impressive rate in the postwar period, and while most long-run studies predicted even greater demands for its services and perhaps larger deficits in the seventies, the actual balance and the full employment balance in the state and local government sector budget had been remarkably stable over the period.

From 1929 to 1969 (excluding World War II years), there was no discernible trend in the balance between receipts and expenditures for the state and local sector in the NIA accounts. In nineteen of those thirty-seven years, the sector showed a surplus, and in eighteen years it showed a deficit. In only one year (1958) did the deficit or surplus exceed $2 billion and in that year the deficit was $2,335 million. In general, the trust funds (mostly state and local employee retirement funds) showed a steadily growing surplus. On the other hand, there was a growing deficit in the general account despite year-to-year fluctuations. The data are given in Table 1-1. It will be noted that even a large "miss" in forecasting expenditures was not of serious consequence in forecasting total demand, since it would usually be offset by a "miss" in forecasting receipts.

Since 1969, however, the state and local government sector has, on the whole, exhibited a different behavior pattern from what it exhibited before 1969. As is shown in Table 1-2, the overall surplus in the national income accounts increased from $0.7 billion in 1969 to $12.3 billion in 1972. The change reflected not only continued increases in the trust fund surplus—from $5.7 billion in 1969 to

### Table 1–1

SURPLUS IN THE STATE AND LOCAL SECTOR, NATIONAL INCOME ACCOUNTS, 1929–1969

($ millions)

| Year | Trust Fund Surplus | Balance on General Govt. Acct. | Overall Surplus or Deficit (−) | Year | Trust Fund Surplus | Balance on General Govt. Acct. | Overall Surplus or Deficit (−) |
|---|---|---|---|---|---|---|---|
| 1929 | 62 | − 255 | − 193 | 1951 | 805 | −1,244 | − 437 |
| 1930 | 69 | − 666 | − 597 | 1952 | 926 | − 967 | − 41 |
| 1931 | 73 | − 824 | − 751 | 1953 | 998 | − 852 | 146 |
| 1932 | 81 | − 361 | − 280 | 1954 | 1,174 | −2,282 | −1,108 |
| 1933 | 86 | − 155 | − 69 | 1955 | 1,255 | −2,525 | −1,270 |
| 1934 | 93 | 368 | 451 | 1956 | 1,384 | −2,253 | − 869 |
| 1935 | 103 | 451 | 554 | 1957 | 1,540 | −2,893 | −1,353 |
| 1936 | 107 | 384 | 491 | 1958 | 1,691 | −4,026 | −2,335 |
| 1937 | 124 | 580 | 704 | 1959 | 1,906 | −2,714 | − 808 |
| 1938 | 137 | 228 | 365 | 1960 | 2,146 | −1,926 | 230 |
| 1939 | 150 | − 118 | 32 | 1961 | 2,291 | −2,813 | − 552 |
| 1940 | 160 | 478 | 638 | 1962 | 2,516 | −1,580 | 936 |
| 1941 | 168 | 1,124 | 1,292 | 1963 | 2,773 | −1,586 | 1,186 |
| 1946 | 308 | 1,585 | 1,893 | 1964 | 3,092 | −1,416 | 1,676 |
| 1947 | 362 | 655 | 1,017 | 1965 | 3,387 | −2,425 | 962 |
| 1948 | 473 | − 399 | 134 | 1966 | 3,728 | −2,462 | 1,266 |
| 1949 | 550 | −1,273 | − 723 | 1967 | 4,300 | −6,099 | −1,799 |
| 1950 | 665 | −1,868 | −1,203 | 1968 | 4,975 | −5,321 | − 346 |
| | | | | 1969 | 5,968 | −5,282 | 686 |

**Source:** U.S. Department of Commerce, *The National Income and Product Accounts of the United States, 1929-1965,* pp. 54-55 and 58-59, and U.S. Department of Commerce, Bureau of Economic Analysis, *Survey of Current Business,* various July issues, 1968-1972.

**Table 1–2**

SURPLUS IN THE STATE AND LOCAL SECTOR, NATIONAL INCOME ACCOUNTS, 1969–1970

($ billions)

| Period | Overall Surplus or Deficit (−) | Trust Fund Surplus or Deficit (−) | General Government Surplus or Deficit (−) |
|---|---|---|---|
| Annual data | | | |
| 1969 | .7 | 5.7 | −5.0 |
| 1970 | 1.8 | 6.5 | −4.8 |
| 1971 | 3.4 | 7.2 | −3.9 |
| 1972 | 12.3 | 8.3 | 4.0 |
| 1973 | 9.2 | 9.1 | 0.1 |
| Quarterly data | | | |
| 1973–I | 13.2 | 8.8 | 4.5 |
| 1973–II | 10.4 | 9.0 | 1.3 |
| 1973–III | 8.4 | 9.2 | −0.8 |
| 1973–IV | 4.6 | 9.4 | −4.7 |
| 1974–I | 3.4 | 9.6 | −6.2 |
| 1974–II | 2.4 | N/A | N/A |

**Source:** U.S. Department of Commerce, Bureau of Economic Analysis, *Survey of Current Business*, July 1973 and July 1974 issues.

$8.3 billion in 1972—but also a turnaround in the general government surplus, from a deficit of $5.0 billion in 1969 ($3.9 billion in 1971) to a surplus of $4.0 billion in 1972. In 1973, however, the general government surplus pretty much vanished: the overall surplus of $9.2 billion was virtually accounted for by the $9.1 billion surplus in the trust funds. Moreover, quarterly reports on the overall surplus in 1973 and 1974 suggest that the general government account may have returned to its "normal" deficit balance.

The temporary reversal of pattern in the state and local government sector—particularly the surpluses on general government account—has not gone unnoticed.

Apart from our own work,[1] it may be noted that in a recent article, Gramlich and Galper used a quarterly econometric model to explain

[1] See David J. Ott, Lawrence J. Korb, Thomas Gale Moore, Attiat F. Ott, Rudolph G. Penner, and Thomas Vasquez, *Nixon, McGovern and the Federal Budget*

the behavior of the general government surplus or deficit of the state and local sector from 1969 to 1972. Their model accurately concluded that the turnaround in the general government account was transitory —that state and local governments would eventually use up the general government surplus by cutting taxes and increasing outlays, as they did by 1973.[2] Their model suggests that "in the long run . . . the surplus does not respond at all to outside forces."[3] They argue persuasively that in 1972 states and localities were in the process of adjusting to unexpectedly large grants-in-aid (particularly general revenue sharing) and to demographic factors (the decline in numbers of school children), and that the general government account showed a temporary surplus during this adjustment period. On this showing, a long-run overall surplus in the state and local government sector would mainly reflect a long-run surplus in the trust funds.

In this volume, we present an analysis of the fiscal behavior of the state and local government sector and we attempt to use the analytical framework to suggest some possible paths for this sector through 1980. A model of the general government account is developed in Chapter 2. Chapter 3 summarizes salient characteristics of state and local retirement funds and, in Chapter 4, a crude but useful actuarial model is used to explore alternative outcomes for the trust fund surplus or deficit in future years. The final chapter uses the 1974 AEI Budget and Resource Allocation Projection Model (BRAP) (after revision of the state and local government sector to incorporate the findings of the present study) to simulate the budget position of the sector during the 1976–1980 period assuming a federal budget path consistent with the fiscal year 1975 budget.

---

(Washington, D. C.: American Enterprise Institute, 1972), pp. 22-25, and David J. Ott, Lawrence J. Korb, Thomas Gale Moore, Dave M. O'Neill, Attiat F. Ott, Rudolph G. Penner, and Thomas Vasquez, *Public Claims on U.S. Output: Federal Budget Options in the Last Half of the Seventies* (Washington, D. C.: American Enterprise Institute, 1973), Chapter 1.

[2] Edward M. Gramlich and Harvey Galper, "State and Local Fiscal Behavior and Federal Grant Policy," in Arthur M. Okun and George L. Perry, eds., *Brookings Papers on Economic Activity*, no. 1 (Washington, D. C.: The Brookings Institution, 1973), pp. 15-58; E. Gramlich, "State and Local Governments and Their Budget Constraint," *International Economic Review*, January 1969; "Alternative Federal Policies for Stimulating State and Local Expenditures: A Comparison of Their Effects," *National Tax Journal*, June 1968.

[3] Gramlich and Galper, "State and Local Fiscal Behavior," p. 47.

# 2

# THE GENERAL GOVERNMENT SECTOR

*Attiat F. Ott and David J. Ott*

It is convenient to analyze the overall activity of state and local governments from the two perspectives of (1) the general government account and (2) the trust fund account. This chapter examines the forces influencing the behavior of the general government account of the state and local government sector. The first section explains the items that make up receipts and expenditures in the national income accounts (NIA) version of the general government account and compares the Census and the NIA surplus or deficit in the general account. The second section develops the general government sector model. The estimates for the equations comprising the model are presented in the third section.

## The General Government Accounts

Table 2–1 gives estimates of the receipts, expenditures and the surplus of the state and local government sector on general government account during calendar 1972, as prepared by the Bureau of Economic Analysis, U.S. Department of Commerce.

As the right side of Table 2–1 indicates, state and local general government expenditures consist of (1) *current account* expenditures for purchases of goods and services (subdivided here into education and noneducation expenditures), transfer payments to persons, mostly for aid to families with dependent children (AFDC), interest paid on

The authors wish to thank Debbie Ott of Data Resources, Inc., for her work in running the regression equations and James J. Breen of Clark University for his assistance in incorporating the state and local sector model into the AEI-BRAP model. Neither is, of course, responsible for analysis and conclusions presented here.

## Table 2–1

STATE AND LOCAL GOVERNMENT RECEIPTS AND EXPENDITURES ON GENERAL GOVERNMENT ACCOUNT, 1972

($ millions)

| Receipts | | Expenditures | |
|---|---|---|---|
| Personal tax and nontax receipts | 34,288 | Current account expenditures | 129,349 |
| Income taxes | 17,460 | Purchases of goods and services | 117,696 |
| Death and gift taxes | 1,443 | Education | 56,181 |
| Motor vehicle licenses | 1,865 | Other | 61,515 |
| Property taxes | 1,380 | Transfer payments to persons | 12,787 |
| Other taxes | 442 | AFDC | 6,876 |
| Nontaxes | 11,698 | Other categorical assistance | 3,365 |
| Corporate profits tax accruals | 4,857 | General assistance | 741 |
| Indirect business tax and nontax accruals | 89,626 | Other | 1,805 |
| Sales tax | 35,578 | Net interest paid | 3,435 |
| State | 31,029 | Subsidies less current surplus of government enterprises | −4,420 |
| Local | 4,549 | Subsidies | 44 |
| Motor vehicle licenses | 1,763 | Surplus | 4,464 |
| Property taxes | 42,703 | Less: Wage accruals less disbursements | −149 |
| Other taxes | 8,012 | Capital account expenditures | 32,677 |
| Nontaxes | 1,570 | Construction | 26,357 |
| Federal grants-in-aid | 37,677 | Education | 5,742 |
| | | Highways[a] | 10,617 |
| | | Other | 9,998 |
| | | Equipment | 6,320 |
| | | Education | 2,585 |
| | | Other | 3,735 |
| TOTAL RECEIPTS | 166,448 | TOTAL EXPENDITURES | 162,324 |
| | | Surplus or deficit (−) | 4,124 |

[a] Includes construction force account compensation.

**Source:** U.S. Department of Commerce, Bureau of Economic Analysis, *Survey of Current Business,* July 1973, Table 3.3, and unpublished Bureau of Economic Analysis data.

state and local debt outstanding, subsidies less current surplus of government enterprises, and other minor items; and (2) *capital account* expenditures for construction (subdivided into highways, education and other) and equipment. On the revenue side, receipts include (1) *personal tax and nontax receipts* (largely income taxes and certain "nontaxes" such as college tuition payments); (2) *corporate profits* tax accruals; (3) *indirect business taxes* (dominated by sales taxes and property taxes); and (4) *federal grants-in-aid.*

The national income accounts (NIA) version of the state and local general government sector is used in developing the model later in this chapter, since the NIA accounts provide the common data base for most economic forecasting, and since the general government model is designed to fit into the AEI Budget and Resource Allocation Projection Model.[1] However, many scholars who work with the state and local government sector use Census data. Table 2–2 provides a reconciliation of the Census general government accounts surplus or deficit with the NIA accounts for fiscal year 1971, the latest year for which the reconciliation items were available at the time of this writing.

**Table 2–2**

DIFFERENCES BETWEEN THE CENSUS GENERAL GOVERNMENT SURPLUS OR DEFICIT (−) AND THE NIA SURPLUS OR DEFICIT, FISCAL YEAR 1971

($ billions)

| | | |
|---|---|---|
| Census general government surplus or deficit (−) | | −6.7 |
| Plus: Net purchases of land | | 1.8 |
| Purchases | 2.0 | |
| Sales | 0.2 | |
| Plus: Adjustment to certain grants-in-aid | | .6 |
| Less: Financial transactions in receipts | | − .2 |
| Plus: Timing differences in expenditure receipts | | 1.1 |
| Equals: NIA general government surplus or deficit | | −3.6 |

**Source:** Computed from data in Bureau of the Census, *Governmental Finances in 1970-71* (Washington, D. C.: Government Printing Office, 1972), p. 18, and from U.S. Department of Commerce, Bureau of Economic Analysis, *Survey of Current Business*, July 1973, Table 3.13.

[1] Paul N. Courant, William H. Branson, Attiat F. Ott, and Roy Wyscarver, *AEI's Budget and Resource Allocation Projection Model* (Washington, D. C.: American Enterprise Institute, 1973).

As Table 2–2 shows, the NIA deficit is smaller than the Census deficit. Most of the difference of $3.1 billion results from the exclusion of land sales from receipts and land purchases from expenditures in the NIA accounts ($1.8 billion) and adjustments in the timing of receipts and expenditures ($1.1 billion). In general, the NIA budget will always show a larger surplus or smaller deficit than the Census data because of positive net land purchases by the sector. The timing adjustment can be either positive or negative. The capital account shown in Table 2–1 is less than the capital account as customarily defined because land transactions are not included.

It may be noted that the NIA data on equipment outlays were of dubious quality until the late 1960s. In the discussions that follow, we define the capital account as consisting of purchases of new and used structures by the state and local sector—that is, as expenditures for construction as shown in Table 2–1 ($26.4 billion).

## A Model of the General Government Sector

A theoretical discussion of the general government model is necessarily formal and somewhat tedious. The reader interested primarily in the implications of the model for the future financial outlook of the state and local government sector can proceed directly to Chapter 5, where the major characteristics of the model are made clear by the simulation results.

**Theoretical Foundations.** In general, there are two approaches one might take in analyzing the behavior of state and local governments. The first approach—the median voter hypothesis—assumes that individuals are the relevant entities to be considered and that all individuals are capable of choosing rationally. In its simplest form, the hypothesis has been stated by James Buchanan as follows:

> If no limits are placed on the number of proposals that may be put forward for a vote . . . [and] under a decision rule of simple majority . . . [t]he predicted outcome will be that indicated to be "most preferred" by the persons whose preferences are median for the whole group. This analysis suggests that because of the median man construction, some analysis of collective decision making under majority rule is possible even if we remain at the level of the individual decision.[2]

[2] J. M. Buchanan, *Public Finance in Democratic Process* (Chapel Hill, N. C.: University of North Carolina Press, 1967), p. 148.

Accordingly, the demand of the individual (the representative or "median voter") for state and local government goods represents the public demand for these goods.[3] The quantity demanded by the "median voter" and supplied by municipalities will be available for all consumers in the municipalities. The use made of the public commodity by any consumer would depend on the nature of the "publicness" of the good. A "pure" public good would be capable of being consumed in equal quantity by all—one individual's consumption would not reduce the good's usefulness to others. Other publicly supplied goods may, however, exhibit some "private" elements in their consumption and "crowding" effects may appear when the goods are shared. The "median voter" approach is based on utility maximization for the individual and the individual is assumed to derive utility from both public consumption and private consumption. His demand function is found by the maximization of utility subject to his budget constraint.

The second approach also uses standard utility analysis, except that the state and local governments or their officials are the units whose utility function is to be maximized. The assumption here is that state and local officials (as distinct from the individual citizen) have a preference function which, although in some way representing the utility functions of the citizens, is not necessarily the same as that of the median individual.[4] State and local government utility functions (or the utility functions of their officials) are then constructed with the usual private and public good arguments, but the budget constraint includes variables—such as statutory constraints on state and local borrowing—not usually found in the individual utility function. The budget constraint is that of the state and local units and not that of the individual.

An alternative to the utility maximization approach would be the use of trend analysis to project state and local government outlays and receipts. In two studies undertaken by the Tax Foundation, Inc. (in 1966 and 1972), general government expenditures and receipts for the state and local sector were projected on the basis of demographic

---

[3] See J. M. Buchanan and G. Tullock, *The Calculus of Consent* (Ann Arbor: University of Michigan Press, 1962); Tullock, *Towards a Mathematics of Politics* (Ann Arbor: University of Michigan Press, 1967); and A. Downs, *An Economic Theory of Democracy* (New York: Harper and Row, 1957).

[4] Edward M. Gramlich and Harvey Galper, "State and Local Fiscal Behavior and Federal Grant Policy," in Arthur M. Okun and George L. Perry, eds., *Brookings Papers on Economic Activity*, no. 1 (Washington, D. C.: The Brookings Institution, 1973), pp. 15-58.

trends and the past experience of the sector.[5] In this approach, the estimates are not based on behavioral equations and therefore important effects of policy on outlays or receipts are not captured. For example, the path of state and local government construction outlays is particularly sensitive to assumptions made about inflation, since inflation affects the rate of interest. Moreover, since past trends in population growth and school enrollment may not be reflected in future experience because of the decline in fertility rates, state and local outlays based on these trends might not be valid at all.

In this study, we adopt the "median voter" approach in analyzing state and local government behavior. We follow the work of Buchanan and Tullock in asserting that "collective action, along with private action, is motivated by individually-conceived ends, and all action proceeds only after a mental calculus is performed by some individual or individuals." [6] We assume that government is elected by majority rule and that competition among political units leads to the election of a government that chooses a budget platform identical to the optimal position of the median voter.[7] With state and local government expenditures responding in this way to the demands of the median voter, taxes and borrowing are determined in a sort of "second stage" where the statutory budget constraints must be met by the governmental unit.

The "median voter" preference model can only be applied straightforwardly to purchases of goods and services on current account (Table 2–1 above), inasmuch as goods and services supplied on current account are closely related to the demands of present voters, while the services supplied by capital reflect in part the decisions of past generations of voters. It is impossible to specify the appropriate "tax price" for the services of state and local capital, and even if it were possible, the necessary data on state and local government stocks of capital and flows of services would still be lacking.[8]

The following sections discuss in turn the median voter model of expenditures on the current account and the equations used to explain expenditures on the capital account (construction).

---

[5] *The Fiscal Outlook for State and Local Government to 1975* (New York: Tax Foundation, Inc., 1966), and *The Financial Outlook for State and Local Government to 1980* (New York: Tax Foundation, Inc., 1972).

[6] Buchanan and Tullock, *Calculus of Consent*, p. 316.

[7] T. E. Borcherding and R. T. Deacon, "The Demand for the Services of Non-Federal Governments," *American Economic Review*, December 1972, pp. 891-901.

[8] Two points should be made here: (1) state and local governments may not always strictly observe the capital/current account distinction and (2) the capital account should include durables as well as construction. However, most writers are willing to accept the capital/current account distinction.

**Expenditures on Current Account.** The first part of the general government sector to be looked at is the part made up of current account expenditures for purchases of goods and services.

*Purchases of goods and services.* The following assumptions have been made in the application of the "median voter" approach to purchases of goods and services on current account:[9]

(1) We assume that current account purchases are those that would be chosen by the median voter as the result of utility maximization. In any year, the state and local government sector is assumed to be able to supply two kinds of current account goods and services—those for education and those for other purchases. The per-unit cost of the social good is assumed to remain the same in any year, regardless of the quantity demanded by the median voter, but the per-unit cost need not be the same over time.

(2) For each consumer $i$ there is a tax share $J_i$ such that $i$ pays the fraction $J_i$ of the total cost of expenditures in the state or locality.

(3) Any consumer $i$ living in any state or local government unit is aware of his tax price $J_iP_i$ for each class of commodity supplied by the state or local unit.

(4) The price of the public good $P_i$ is equal to its marginal (average) cost.

(5) Federal grants to state and local governments are perceived by the consumer as affecting the price of the public good he demands by reducing his tax share without any effect on his income. Only their price effects on individual demand are considered.

(6) The quantity of any good supplied by any state or local government unit is the quantity demanded by the median voter.

(7) State and local real purchases represent the goods demanded by the median voter. Other current account expenditures, such as transfer payments for public assistance and interest paid, do not enter the individual utility function and are treated separately.

(8) The "publicness" of state and local commodities affects the relation between population and individual demands. The extent to which goods are jointly consumed may be determined by the parameter $\gamma$. The value of $\gamma$ would presumably range from zero

[9] See Borcherding and Deacon, "Demand for Services of Non-Federal Governments."

in the case of a jointly consumed good (if no one is excluded from consumption) to one in the case of a good whose consumption benefits only the user.[10]

(9) "Spill-ins" and "spill-outs" are ignored. The median voter either discounts the flow of benefits spilled into his community from purchases made by other communities or he treats such inflows as substitutes for the outflows from his community to others.

Now let us consider the model that follows from these assumptions. Current account purchases of goods and services are divided into two categories, education purchases (*GSLCE*) and other purchases (*GSLCO*). Let the quantities of state and local current account purchases be

$$Z_1 = \frac{GSLCE}{PEC} = \text{real education purchases}$$

$$Z_2 = \frac{GSLCO}{POC} = \text{real other purchases}$$

where

*PEC* is the implicit price deflator for education purchases (1958 = 1.0)

*POC* is the implicit price deflation for other purchases (1958 = 1.0), and

let

$Z_3$ be a basket of goods containing both real personal private consumption and savings and the quantity of federally provided public goods.

The median individual is assumed to maximize the utility function

$$U = U\,(Z_1^*, Z_2^*, Z_3^*) \tag{2.1}$$

where

$Z_i^*$ denotes the quantity of good $i$ the individual treats as giving rise to utility—allowing for the "crowding effect" on utility. $Z^*$ is defined as

$$Z_1^* = \frac{Z_1}{N\gamma} = N^{-\gamma} Z_1 \tag{2.1a}$$

[10] For estimates of the value of the crowding parameter, see T. C. Bergstrom and R. P. Goodman, "Private Demands for Public Goods," *American Economic Review*, June 1973, pp. 280-96.

$$Z_2^* = \frac{Z_2}{N\gamma} = N^{-\gamma}Z_2 \tag{2.1b}$$

$$Z_3^* = \frac{Z_3}{N\gamma} = N^{-\gamma}Z_3 \tag{2.1c}$$

The constraint is

$$P_3Z_3 + JEPECZ_1 + JOPOCZ_2 = Y/N \tag{2.2}$$

where

$N$ = population sharing the good with the individual,
$JEPEC$ = tax price of current account education purchases,
$JOPOC$ = tax price of current account noneducation purchases,
$P_3$ = a composite price index for private consumption and saving and for public goods provided by the federal government, and
$Y/N$ = the median voter's income (where the mean is used as a proxy for the median value).

The median voter's constraint is that his expenditures on private and public goods cannot exceed his income. Maximizing (2.1) subject to (2.2) yields demand functions for $Z_1^*$, $Z_2^*$, and $Z_3^*$. The quantity of the $i^{th}$ state and local government public good demand is $N\gamma Z_i^*$. The tax price of this public good $i$—$J_iP_i$—is defined as

$$J_iP_i = \frac{(1 - M_i)}{N} P_i \tag{2.5}$$

where

$M_i$ = the federal grant matching rate for this type good,
$N$ = the population sharing the tax cost with the individual, and
$P_i$ = the price deflator for this type of state and local current account purchase (a proxy for the marginal cost of the public commodity). Thus $\frac{(1 - M_i)}{N} P_i$ may be thought of as the subsidized price of the $i^{th}$ public good as perceived by the median voter.

The system of demand equations would then have the form

$$Z_1 = Z_1\,(Y/N, JEPEC, JOPOC, P_3, N) \tag{2.6a}$$

$$Z_2 = Z_2\,(Y/N, JEPEC, JOPOC, P_3, N) \tag{2.6b}$$

$$Z_3 = Z_3\,(Y/N, JEPEC, JOPOC, P_3, N). \tag{2.6c}$$

The sum of the coefficients of the $Y/N$ variable should be unity—that is, a change in $Y/N$ should be just "used up" by some combination of changes in consumption of the $Z$'s and the price variables should have coefficients summing to zero.

The equations for *GSLCE* and *GSLCO* used here are based on the form suggested by the median preference model. However, since the system is not truly simultaneous because construction outlays are omitted and $P_3$ cannot be readily estimated, relative price effects were ignored and the estimates were of the form:

$$GSLCE = f\,(Y/N, PEC, JE, N) \tag{2.7}$$

$$GSLCO = f\,(Y/N, POC, JO, N)\,. \tag{2.8}$$

*PEC* and *POC* refer to estimates of the current account deflators for education and other purchases.[11] In the present study, these "supply prices" were obtained from equations of the general form

$$PEC = F\,(\Delta\, EPOP, WE) \tag{2.9}$$

$$POC = f\,(CRIME, WO) \tag{2.10}$$

where

$\Delta EPOP$ = change in the number of students enrolled in public schools,

*WE* = average wage per public school employee,

*CRIME* = FBI index of crimes committed, and

*WO* = average wage per noneducation state and local employee.

All these variables would be expected to increase the supply price of a unit of education or other state and local services.

*Transfer payments.* State and local government expenditures on transfer payments were assumed to be determined exogenously. While transfer payments for public assistance (*STRFPA*) can be thought of as entering the utility function of the median voter (because the distribution of income affects the individual's utility), at this point we chose to treat such transfers as being exogenous. No demand for transfer payments is estimated for the median voter's utility function.[12]

*Interest.* Interest payments made on the general government account (*SINTGG*) come from past borrowings and thus in any period

[11] See J. C. Ohls and T. J. Wales, "Supply and Demand for State and Local Services," *Review of Economics and Statistics,* vol. 54 (November 1972), pp. 424-30.

[12] For debate over attempts to make the distribution of income a part of the individual utility function, see Lester Thurow, "The Income Distribution as a Pure Public Good," *Quarterly Journal of Economics,* May 1971, pp. 327-35; and "Comments" by several writers in the May 1973 issue of the same journal.

are a predetermined variable. Although the median voter implicitly determines borrowing on general government account—for meeting expenditures not entirely financed by taxes—the amount of interest paid depends on past commitments (reflecting the choices of past voters) as well as on the borrowing rate available to the state and local government sector. To estimate interest payments, both past borrowing and past municipal bond rates should enter as explanatory variables. Thus,

$$SINTGG = (D_{-1}, RM_{-1}, RM_{-2} \ldots) \tag{2.11}$$

where

$D_{-1}$ = state and local government debt outstanding at the beginning of the period, and
$RM_{-i}$ = municipal bond rate lagged $i$ periods.

*Subsidies less current surplus of government enterprises.* Subsidies less the current surplus of state and local government enterprises (*SSURPE*) is entered as a negative item in the expenditure side of the NIA current account. For our study this item is assumed to be exogenously determined. Specifically, *SSURPE* is assumed to grow with nominal GNP.

*Total current account outlays.* Total current account outlays are equal to the sum of current account purchases of goods and services, transfer payments and interest with subsidies less current surplus of government enterprises subtracted from the total—or

$$GSCL + GSLCE + GSLCO + STRFPA + SINTGG - SSURPE. \tag{2.12}$$

**Structures Purchases.** In addition to current account goods and services supplied by state and local governments, individuals enjoy services from the stock of state and local capital. Schools, roads, sewers, and so on, all provide a flow of current benefits to users. Ideally, using the median voter model, one would want to be able to explain the optimum flow of capital services and thus the desired stock of capital. But this cannot really be done. For one thing, the median voter demand is for a *flow* of capital services during a given period. Since the existing stock of state and local capital is the result of past voter decisions over many years, the current flow of services is also the result of these past decisions. The voter in the present period can only affect the future flow of services to the community or the marginal addition (in his lifetime) to the total existing capital stock of state and local governments. In addition, the accumulation of state and local capital, to the extent it is debt-financed, gives rise to a liability which must be partially paid by present households. Because of these timing problems, the flow of services in the current period may or may not equal the amount needed to service the debt outstanding. In other words, the price of capital services the median voter is willing to pay may not be equal to debt retirement plus interest. Finally, good data on the stock of state and local government capital, the depreciation rate (needed to measure capital services), and the appropriate rental price of capital are just not available. For these reasons, purchases of structures were explained in the model eclectically as a function of price, income, federal grants, and some demographic variables.

Total state and local construction equals the sum of required and discretionary construction. Required construction is construction required to receive federal aid, and is determined by the grant funds available and the proportion of each dollar of construction that can be paid for with federal funds (the matching rate). Since the federal matching rate varies for various kinds of construction, total state and local government purchases of structures were subdivided into three components: highway construction (*GSLIH*), education construction (*GSLIE*), and other construction (*GSLIO*). The general form of the structure purchase equations is as follows:

$$\frac{GSLI_i}{PI_i58} = f(MI_i, VAID_i, RM, X_i) \tag{2.13}$$

where

$\frac{GSLI_i}{PI_i58}$ = real purchases of type $i$ construction (1958 dollars),

$MI_i$ = the federal matching rate,

$VAID_i$ = federal construction grants for the $i^{\text{th}}$ category,

$RM$ = the state and local government borrowing rate, and

$X_i$ = the appropriate demographic variable (s).

Total real construction purchases is then equal to

$$\frac{GSLI}{PI58} = \frac{GSLIH}{PIH58} + \frac{GSLIE}{PIE58} + \frac{GSLIO}{PIO58} \tag{2.14}$$

and construction expenditure in current dollars is given by

$$GSLI = GSLIH + GSLIE + GSLIO.^{13} \tag{2.15}$$

[13] Actually, outlays for highway construction (*GSLIH*) were estimated in current dollars rather than in real terms because the results were better.

The nominal values for highway construction, education construction and other construction were obtained by multiplying each real quantity by an estimated value of the deflator (*PIH58*, *PIE58*, and *PIO58*). These deflators were estimated from the deflator for producers' structures in the GNP accounts (*PSD58*).

**Total General Government Outlays.** These outlays (*SEGG*) are equal to total current account outlays (equation 2.12) plus structures purchases (equation 2.15).

$$SEGG = GSLCE + GSLCO + GSLI + SINTGG + STRFPA - SSURPE. \quad (2.16)$$

**Taxes.** With current account and construction expenditures estimated, the next step is the estimation of the revenue side of the state and local general government budget. Most macroeconomic models provide independent estimates of the components of receipts—personal tax and nontax receipts, corporate profits taxes, indirect business taxes, and (usually defined as exogenous) federal grants-in-aid. However, this procedure of independent estimation introduces a serious problem. It is difficult, with so many different state tax systems, to separate revenue changes resulting from legislation from revenue changes resulting from growth in the tax base. In fact, most estimating equations reflect the past pattern of revenue growth which reflects both legislation and economic growth.

However, the median voter approach used here provides a way out of this difficulty. The expenditure estimates already reflect, through the "tax price," the taxes the median man is willing to pay. With assumptions made about the budget constraint of individual state and local units, about their behavior in financing construction, and about the path of federal grants, the expenditure estimates can be used to generate the revenue estimates and the resulting general government surplus or deficit.

*Taxes to finance the current account.* Since state and local governments are generally required to raise taxes in order to finance all current account expenditures not financed by grants and to cover debt retirement and interest and planned acquisition of financial assets, current account taxes (*TAXC*) are assumed to be equal to

$$TAXC = GSLCE + GSLCO + SINTGG + STRFPA - VAIDC - SSURPE + DRET + \Delta A \quad (2.17)$$

where

$VAIDC$ = total grants for current account expenditures,
$STRFPA$ = transfer payments for public assistance,
$SINTGG$ = interest payments,
$SSURPE$ = subsidy less current surplus of state and local government enterprises,
$DRET$ = long-term debt to be retired in the current period, and
$\Delta A$ = the net acquisition of financial assets during the current period.

General revenue sharing poses special problems. Should general revenue-sharing grants be treated as current or capital account grants? Within broad limits, they can be used for either purpose. While the Office of Revenue Sharing of the U.S. Treasury Department is collecting "use reports" on how these funds are used, thus far only eighteen-months' experience is available. This limited experience suggests that 34 percent of the general revenue-sharing fund actually spent in 1972 and 1973 went for capital outlays.[14] For lack of better evidence, this figure was used here to allocate general revenue sharing among current account grants and capital account grants. The figure for $VAIDC$ thus includes 66 percent of the general revenue-sharing funds for each year.

Long-term debt to be retired in each period is predetermined. In the model we estimated it in general form as a function of long-term debt outstanding at the end of the previous year:

$$DRET = f(D_{-1}). \qquad (2.18)$$

To obtain a value for long-term debt outstanding at the end of each period, debt outstanding was defined as equal to the last period's debt outstanding *plus* new borrowing ($B$) *less* debt retirement ($DRET$):

$$D = D_{-1} + B - DRET. \qquad (2.19)$$

New issues of long-term debt were then assumed to be a function of construction expenditures not financed by grants ($GSLI - VAIDI$), the municipal bond rate ($RM$) and the ratio of financial assets to long-term debt outstanding ($A/D$) at the beginning of the period. It is presumed that the greater the amount of construction not financed by grants, the greater the volume of borrowing will be. Also, the greater the municipal bond rate, the lower the amount that will be borrowed to finance construction. Also the amount borrowed will be lower the greater the asset/debt ratio (that is, more use will be made

[14] *Budget of the United States Government, Fiscal Year 1975* (Washington, D. C.: Government Printing Office, 1974).

of existing liquid assets to finance construction). The general form of the equation for $B$ is thus assumed to be

$$B = f(GSLI - VAIDI), RM, A_{-1}/D_{-1}). \quad (2.20)$$

Since the borrowing equation introduces a new variable $A$, the net financial assets of state and local governments (that is, financial assets of general government less short-term debt), this variable must also be estimated. By analogy to the transactions demand for money,[15] $A$ was assumed to be a positive function of total general government expenditures ($SEGG$) and a negative function of the municipal bond rate ($RM$). Thus

$$A = f(SEGG, RM). \quad (2.21)$$

*Taxes to finance construction.* Given the assumption on current account taxes, tax receipts available to finance construction ($TAXI$) would be equal to total general government tax receipts, $STAXGG$, less current account taxes, $TAXC$. Thus

$$TAXI = STAXGG - TAXC. \quad (2.22)$$

Since state and local government construction, $GSLI$, is financed partly by construction grants ($VAIDI$), partly by new borrowing ($B$), partly by a change in assets ($A$), and partly by taxes, $TAXI$ should be a function of construction outlays not financed by federal grants, of the change in financial assets held by state and local governments, and of the municipal bond rate. Thus

$$TAXI = f(GSLI - VAIDI), \Delta A, RM). \quad (2.23)$$

As noted earlier, a portion of general revenue sharing is included in grants for construction ($VAIDI$).

*The allocation of taxes by type of tax.* Thus far we have determined total taxes on general government account ($STAXGG$) to be

$$STAXGG = TAXC + TAXI. \quad (2.24)$$

Total current account taxes ($TAXC$) are assumed to equal current account outlay for goods and services, transfer payments, interest, debt retirement, increments to assets after deduction of the portion financed by federal grants, and surpluses of enterprises (equation 2.17). Taxes for construction ($TAXI$) as explained by equation (2.23)

[15] William J. Baumol, "Transactions Demand for Cash: An Inventory Theoretic Approach," *Quarterly Journal of Economics*, November 1952, pp. 545-56, and *Economic Theory and Operations Analysis* (Englewood Cliffs, New Jersey: Prentice-Hall, 1964), pp. 3-11, 241-45. For an application to the state-local sector, see J. Richard Aronson, "The Idle Cash Balances of State and Local Governments," *Journal of Finance*, vol. 23 (June 1968), pp. 499-500.

depend on construction expenditures not financed by grants, on the change in assets (which substitute for *TAXI*), and on the cost of borrowing for construction as opposed to financing it through taxation (that is, the municipal bond rate).[16]

To integrate the state and local general government model with the AEI-BRAP model (see Chapter 5 below), it is necessary to break down *STAXGG* by major type of tax—personal tax and nontax payments (*STPNIA*), corporate profits tax accruals (*SCT*), and indirect business taxes (*SIBT*), which include property taxes and sales taxes. It is of course difficult to separate changes in tax revenues that reflect legislative action from changes in tax revenues that reflect changes in economic conditions and thus the tax base. In general, state and local personal and corporate income taxes are sensitive to the business cycle, while indirect business taxes (especially property taxes) are much less sensitive. Therefore, in the projection of state and local taxes into the future, we first allowed personal and corporate taxes to run off GNP[17] and corporate profits, respectively, assuming elasticities with respect to the base for each tax (1.1 for personal taxes and 1.0 for corporate taxes) that are roughly consistent with no rate increases.[18] Given personal and corporate taxes, state-local indirect business taxes were then assumed to fill the gap between *STAXGG* and the sum of *STPNIA* and *SCT*. Thus, simulation of the general government model does not necessarily produce accurate estimates of individual types of state and local taxes, but only of the overall magnitude of these taxes. This procedure has the advantage of allowing analysis of the pressures on the rates in the future, a major source of concern to state and local officials and taxpayers.

**The NIA Deficit or Surplus.** Now, having discussed general government expenditures and revenues, let us consider the components of the general government surplus or deficit on a national income accounts basis. The general government surplus (*SSURPGG*) is equal

[16] Alternatively, as shown below, *STAXGG* can be obtained more directly with an equation which estimates the general government surplus or deficit (−) which is then added to expenditures (*SEGG*) less grants (*VAID*) to get *STAXGG*. That is, $STAXGG = SSURPGG + SEGG - VAID$.

Knowing *SEGG* and *SSURPGG* on the right side, we know *STAXGG*, since grants are assumed to be exogenous.

[17] Personal taxable income (*YPT* in the BRAP model) is equal to personal income less transfer payments (which are not taxable) plus personal contributions for social insurance (which is included in income subject to tax but not in personal income).

[18] See Advisory Commission on Intergovernmental Relations, *Federal-State-Local Finances: Significant Features of Fiscal Federalism*, 1973-74 edition (Washington, D. C.: U.S. Government Printing Office, 1974), p. 320.

to general government revenues (*SREVGG*) less general government expenditures:

$$SSURPGG = SREVGG - SEGG \tag{2.25}$$

where

$$\begin{aligned} SREVGG &= STAXGG + VAID \\ SREVGG &= TAXC + TAXI + VAID. \end{aligned} \tag{2.26}$$

Writing out the components of *TAXC* and *SEGG*, we get

$$\begin{aligned} SSURPGG &= GSLC + SINTGG + STRFPA - VAIDC \\ &- SSURPE + DRET + \Delta A + TAXI + VAID - GSLCE \\ &+ GSLCO - GSLI - SINTGG - STRFPA + SSURPE. \end{aligned} \tag{2.27}$$

Cancelling terms, we reduce the equation to

$$SSURPGG = VAIDI + DRET + \Delta A + TAXI - GSLI \tag{2.28}$$

or

$$SSURPGG = DRET + \Delta A - (GSLI - VAIDI - TAXI). \tag{2.29}$$

The last term represents net borrowing for construction (*NBC*)—that is, the portion of construction not financed by grants or taxes. This reduces the surplus on the general government account. Debt retirement and asset acquisition, on the other hand, add to the surplus.

The general government surplus or deficit on an NIA basis reflects the relation between net borrowing for construction (*NBC*) and debt retirement and the change in financial assets. As long as state and local governments borrow more to finance construction than $DRET + \Delta A$, they will show a general government deficit. If, however, construction changes so that debt retirement plus the change in financial assets exceeds *NBC*, then the general government accounts will show a surplus.

## The Estimated Equations

Table 2–3 summarizes the results of the estimates of the equations for the general government model discussed above. The regression equations used are generally based on annual time series data for the period 1952–1971 (in a few cases for 1954–1971) and are ordinary least-square regressions. (The estimated equations and sources of data are contained in an appendix to the chapter.)

The results shown in the table suggest that the price elasticity of real current account purchases varies between −0.139 for education and −0.414 for other purchases, indicating what one might expect—a low price elasticity for the demand for education as against the demand for other state and local services. For education, both the

**Table 2–3**

SUMMARY OF COEFFICIENTS FOR EQUATIONS IN THE GENERAL GOVERNMENT MODEL

(Estimating period 1952-1971)

| Independent Variables | Dependent Variables | | | | | |
|---|---|---|---|---|---|---|
| | log *GSLCE/EPOP* | log *GSLCO* | *GSLIE/PIE*58 | *GSLIH* | *GSLIO/PIO*58 | *TAXI* |
| Per capita income, lagged [log $(Y/N)_{-1}$] | .411 | 1.311 | | | | |
| Tax share for education (log *JE*) | −.947 | | | | | |
| Price deflator for current education purchases (log *PEC*58) | .861 | | | | | |
| Price deflator for other current purchases (*POC*58) | | .586 | | | | |
| Population (log *N*) | | .919 | | | | |
| Population lagged one period ($N_{-1}$) | | | | | 113.3 | |
| 1/federal matching rate for highways (*MH*) | | | | 14559.4 | | |
| Highways construction grants lagged $(VAIDIH)_{-1}$ | | | | 1.410 | | |
| Construction outlays not financed by grants | | | | | | .000302 |
| Aaa municipal borrowing rate (*RM*) | | | | | −926.1 | |
| Aaa municipal borrowing rate lagged ($RM_{-1}$) | | | −405.7 | | | |

| | | |
|---|---|---|
| Change in state and local financial assets ($\Delta A$) | | −.641 |
| Public enrollment in elementary & secondary & higher education, lagged ($EPOP_{-1}$) | .101 | |
| Residual ($RHO$) | .599 | |

**Source:** Authors' estimates. All expenditure and grants-in-aid variables in millions of dollars. Population in millions, interest rate in percent terms.

tax share and income were significant, with the appropriate signs. The best estimates for debt retirement (*DRET*) and interest payments (*SINTGG*) were made with the existing stock of state and local government debt outstanding as the only variable.

For the structures purchases equations, all variables turned out to be significant, with the correct sign. The *TAXI* equation—tax receipts used to finance construction—suggests that, on the average, about 30 percent of construction outlays not financed by grants ($GSLI - VAIDI$) is financed by taxes and that an increase in assets reduces this ratio. The negative sign of the change in state-local net financial assets ($\Delta A$) indicates that more reliance would be placed on *TAXI* as the financial position worsens and less reliance as it improves. The municipal bond rate (*RM*) was not significant.

As the table shows, the only case providing a clue to the magnitude of the parameter $\gamma$ is that of current account outlays other than education, where the coefficient of *N* suggests that these outlays may be largely for goods that are not jointly consumed. *N* did not appear as a significant variable in *GSLCE;* hence it can be inferred that in this case $\gamma$ is not significantly different from zero and public education may thus be considered to be jointly consumed.

## Simulation of the General Government Budget Outlook

To simulate the future path of the state-local sector budget, we must project (1) the federal budget parameters, that is, the level and types of aid and the matching rates, (2) the path of gross national product, personal income per capita, prices, corporate profits, interest rates and the other economic variables, and (3) the path of demographic variables such as public school enrollment (*EPOP*), population (*N*) and crime. Such a simulation, carried out with the AEI-BRAP model, is presented in Chapter 5.

First, however, an effort must be made to deal with the trust funds managed by the state-local sector, whose receipts, expenditures, and surplus figure in the overall NIA budget numbers. The following two chapters deal with this area.

## Appendix to Chapter 2

**Estimated Equations.** The estimated equations used in the general government model are set forth below. The figures in parentheses are *t* values. For the variables estimated in millions of dollars, the estimate is divided by 1,000 to put them in billions of dollars to use in the AEI-BRAP model.

$$PEC58 = \underset{(6.548)}{.153258} - \underset{(-2.275)}{.0000269886 \Delta EPOP} + \underset{(77.944)}{.000203579\,WE} \qquad (E.1)$$

$$\bar{R}^2 = .997$$
$$DW = 1.435$$

$$POC58 = \underset{(.356)}{.0281324} - \underset{(-3.559)}{.0269154\,CRIME} + \underset{(8.219)}{.000302599\,WO} \qquad (E.2)$$

$$\bar{R}^2 = .990$$
$$DW = .829$$

$$\log\left(\frac{GSLCE}{EPOP}\right) = (\underset{(-2.064)}{-2.5369} + \underset{(2.499)}{.411492 \log (Y/N)-1} + \underset{(--3.628)}{.860781}$$

$$\log PEC58 - \underset{(-4.200)}{.94716 \log JE)/1000} \qquad (E.3)$$

$$\bar{R}^2 = .998$$
$$DW = 2.066$$

$$\log GSLCO = (\underset{(-1.903)}{-5.08657} + \underset{(11.539)}{1.31089 \log (Y/N)-1} + \underset{(2.268)}{.585596}$$

$$\log POC58 + \underset{(2.266)}{.918563 \log N)/1000} \qquad (E.4)^*$$

$$\bar{R}^2 = .999$$
$$DW = 1.98$$

$$SINTGG = (\underset{(1.82065)}{171.209} + \underset{(15.5580)}{17.774\,D_{-1}})/1000 \qquad (E.5)$$

$$\bar{R}^2 = .9305$$
$$DW = .6386$$

$$PIE58 = \underset{(-8.616)}{-.189321} + \underset{(62.626)}{1.21401\,PSD58} \qquad (E.6)$$

$$\bar{R}^2 = .995$$
$$DW = .50$$

$$PIH58 = \underset{(-4.206)}{-0.4892} + \underset{(14.137)}{1.48426\,PGNPD58} \qquad (E.7)$$

$$\bar{R}^2 = .904$$
$$DW = .871$$

$$PIO\,58 = \underset{(-3.934)}{-.22431} + \underset{(24.643)}{1.23973\,PSD58} \qquad (E.8)$$

$$\bar{R}^2 = .970$$
$$DW = 1.565$$

---

* The tax price variable *JOPO* was dropped from E.4 for lack of significance.

$$\frac{GSLIE}{PIE58} = \underset{(.39128)}{(443.503} + \underset{(3.124)}{.101004}\ EPOP_{-1} - \underset{(-2.730)}{405.744}\ RM_{-1} \quad \text{(E.9)}$$

$$+ \underset{(2.833)}{.598809}\ RHO)/1000$$

$$\bar{R}^2 = .830$$
$$DW = .913$$

$$GSLIH = \underset{(3.20527)}{(22107.4} - \underset{(-3.04324)}{14559.4}\left(\frac{1}{MH}\right) + \underset{(5.84888)}{1.40962}\ VAIDH_{-1})/1000$$

$$\bar{R}^2 = .918 \quad \text{(E.10)}$$
$$DW = .9547$$

$$GSLIO/PIO58 = \underset{(-6.989)}{(-19470.1} + \underset{(3.566)}{4835.91}\ MIO - \underset{(-4.310)}{926.110}\ RM_{-1} \quad \text{(E.11)}$$

$$+ \underset{(9.288)}{113.271}\ N_{-1})/1000$$

$$\bar{R}^2 = .897$$
$$DW = 1.435$$

$$B = \underset{(1.0045)}{1.80521} + \underset{(8.84)}{.000524093}\ GSLI - \underset{(-.011973)}{.000365712}\ RM \quad \text{(E.12)}$$

$$-\underset{(-1.9587)}{.2929}\ (A_{-1}/D_{-1})$$

$$\bar{R}^2 = .959$$
$$DW = 1.60$$

$$DRET = \underset{(2.292)}{.218105} + \underset{(47.982)}{.0554631}\ D_{-1} \quad \text{(E.13)}$$

$$\bar{R}^2 = .992$$
$$DW = 1.12$$

$$\log A = \underset{(-13.492)}{-6.04412} + \underset{(18.688)}{.90608}\ \log SEGG - \underset{(-4.907)}{.403825}\ \log RM_{-1} \quad \text{(E.14)}$$

$$\bar{R}^2 = .987$$
$$DW = 1.694$$

$$TAXI = \underset{(1.983)}{.727657} + \underset{(9.0276)}{.00030208}\ (GSLI - VAIDI) - \underset{(-6.776)}{.640623}\Delta A$$

$$\bar{R}^2 = .815 \quad \text{(E.15)}$$
$$DW = 2.792$$

$$STPNIA = 1.1\ (GNP/GNP_{-1})\ STPNIA_{-1} \quad \text{(E.16)}$$

$$S = (CP/CP_{-1})\ SCT_{-1} \quad \text{(E.17)}$$

**List of Variables.** The variables in the estimated equations are as follows:

*GSLCE* = current account education purchases (billions of dollars)

*GSLCO* = other current account purchases (billions of dollars)

*WE* = education wages and salaries

*WO* = other wages and salaries

*CRIME* = crime rate per 1,000 population

*PSD58* = state and local purchases deflator (1958 = 1.0)

*PGNPD58* = private GNP deflator (1958 = 1.0)

*PIE58* = price deflator for education construction (1958 = 1.0)

*PIH58* = price deflator for highways construction (1958 = 1.0)

*PIO58* = price deflator for other construction (1958 = 1.0)

*SEGG* = total general government expenditures (billions of dollars)

*STPNIA* = personal tax and nontax payments (billions of dollars)

*SCT* = corporate profits tax accruals (billions of dollars)

*GNP* = gross national product (billions of current dollars)

*CP* = corporate profits

*GSLIE* = real construction outlays for education (billions of 1958 dollars)

*GSLIH* = real construction outlays for highways (billions of 1958 dollars)

*GSLIO* = real construction outlays for all others (billions of 1958 dollars)

*DRET* = debt retirement (billions of dollars)

*TAXI* = taxes to finance construction (billions of dollars)

*SINTGG* = general government interest payments (billions of dollars)

$\frac{Y}{N}$ = per capita personal income (dollars)

*PEC* = price deflator for education purchases in current amount (1958 = 1.0)

*POC* = price deflator for other current account purchases (1958 = 1.0)

*PI* = price deflator for construction purchases (1958 = 1.0)

*EPOP* = public enrollment in elementary and secondary education and higher education (thousands of students)

*RM* = Aaa municipal borrowing rate (percent)

*N* = population (millions of people)

$VAIDIH$ = federal grants for highway construction (millions of dollars)

$VAIDI$ = total federal grants for construction (millions of dollars)

$JE$ = tax share for education ($= \frac{1-g}{N}$ where $(1 - g)$ is per dollar outlays net of grants)

$1/MH$ = reciprocal federal matching rate for highways

$MIO$ = a weighted average of federal matching rate for other construction outlays (percent)

$A$ = state and local government financial assets (billions of dollars)

$D$ = state and local government debt outstanding (billions of dollars)

$RHO$ = residual, lagged one period

For *GSLCE* and *GSLCO*, the coefficient of *PEC* and *POC* on the right-hand side represents $(1 + E)$, where $E$ is the elasticity of real purchases with respect to price, presumably a negative member.

**Sources.** The data are taken from the following sources:

Net assets of state and local governments ($A$): From U.S. Department of Commerce, Bureau of the Census, *Governmental Finances,* annual issues. Computed as financial assets minus short-term debt; fiscal year data converted to calendar year basis.

Gross long-term borrowing ($B$): Same source as for $A$, and also converted from fiscal to calendar year basis.

Long-term debt outstanding ($D$): Same source as for $B$. Initial value of $D$ (1952) grown by $B - DRET$ in each year, after conversion of $B$ and *DRET* to calendar years by averaging the fiscal years.

Long-term debt retired (*DRET*): Same source as for $B$.

Public school enrollment (*EPOP*): Tax Foundation, Inc., *Facts and Figures on Government Finance,* 1971 and 1973 editions.

Current account purchases (*GSLC*): Sum of *GSLCE* and *GSLCO*.

Current account purchases for education (*GSLCE*): Total state-local purchases for education *less* construction outlays for education, from U.S. Department of Commerce, Bureau of Economic Analysis, *Survey of Current Business,* various issues, 1967–1972, and *National Income and Product Accounts of the United States* (Washington, D. C.: U.S. Department of Commerce, Bureau of Economic Analysis, 1966), Table 3.11.

Current account purchases other than education (*GSLCO*): Same source as for *GSLCE;* defined as "other purchases" in Table 3.11 less the construction component of other purchases.

Construction outlays (*GSLI*): Same source as for *GSLCE* and *GSLCO* except from Table 3.3. Excludes construction force account compensation.

Construction outlays for education (*GSLIE):* Same source as for *GSLCE.*

Construction outlays for highways (*GSLIH*): For 1957–1973, from unpublished BEA estimates which include construction force account compensation; for 1952–1957, from Department of Labor and Department of Commerce, "Construction Volume and Costs, 1915–1956," *Statistical Supplement to Construction Review,* 1957.

Construction outlays except education and highways (*GSLIO*): Calculated as *GSLI* less *GSLIE* and *GSLIH.*

Matching rate for grants for education (*ME*): As noted in the text, *ME* is calculated as $(1 - \frac{VAIDE}{GSLCE})/N$, where *VAIDE* is federal grants for education (from *National Income and Product Accounts of the U.S.* and *Survey of Current Business,* various issues, 1967–1973, Table 3.10).

Matching rate for grants for highway construction (1/*MH):* Highway construction grants (*VAIDIH* below) multiplied by the reciprocal of the federal share for each component (that is, grants for the interstate system and grants for the system formerly known as the ABC system), with this total then divided by *VAIDIH.* Federal shares obtained from various issues of *Budget of the United States Government.*

Matching rate for construction other than education and highways (1/*MIO*): Conceptually the same as 1/*MH* above; grants and federal shares for non-highway and education construction obtained from various issues of *Budget of the United States Government,* Special Analysis D, converted to calendar basis.

Population (*N*): U.S. Bureau of the Census, as reported in *Report of the President's Council of Economic Advisers,* February 1974, p. 275.

Deflator for current account state-local education purchases (*PEC58*): Obtained by deflation of the "compensation of employee" and "other purchases" components of current account education purchases (both from the same source as *GSLCE* above) by unpublished BEA deflators for these two types of purchases used by Gramlich and Galper, "State and Local Fiscal Behavior and Federal Grant Policy," in Arthur M. Okun and George L. Perry, eds., *Brookings Papers on Economic Activ-*

*ity,* no. 1 (Washington, D. C.: The Brookings Institution, 1973); deflated total current account education purchases were then divided into current dollar current account purchases to obtain *PEC.*

Deflator for state-local construction outlays for education (*PIE58*): The state-local overall construction deflator used by Gramlich and Galper.

Deflator for state-local highway construction outlays (*PIH58*): The BEA deflator for "public structures: highways and streets," presented in Table 8.7 of the *Survey of Current Business,* and *National Income and Product Accounts of the United States, 1929–65* was used as *PIH.*

Deflator for state-local construction outlays except education and highways (*PIO58*): Obtained as a residual. Deflated "other" construction outlays were obtained by subtracting deflated highway and education construction outlays from total deflated construction outlays. This was then divided into *GSLIO* to obtain the implicit deflator for "other" state-local construction outlays (*PIO58*).

Deflator for "other" current account outlays (*POC58*): Obtained in the same manner and using the same data sources as *PEC58* above.

Municipal bond rate (*RM*): Moodys Aaa bond rate for state and local securities, as reported in various issues of the *Federal Reserve Bulletin.*

Interest paid by state-local general government (*SINTGG*): Obtained as the sum of "net interest paid" by state and local governments (Table 3.3 in the *Survey of Current Business*), plus interest received by state-local trust funds, *SINTTF* (Table 3.7 in the *Survey of Current Business*).

Interest received by state-local trust funds (*SINTTF*): From Table 3.7, *Survey of Current Business,* various issues.

Assets of state-local trust funds (*STFA*): From Department of Commerce, Bureau of the Census, *Governmental Finances,* various issues, adjusted to a calendar year basis.

State transfers for public assistance (*STRFPA*): Difference between total transfer payments by state-local governments (Table 3.3 in the *Survey of Current Business*) and benefits paid by trust funds (Table 3.9 in the *Survey of Current Business*).

Taxes to finance construction (*TAXI*): Obtained as a residual from the definition explained in the text above—that is, $TAXI = SSURPGG - DRET - \Delta A - VAIDI + GSLI$.

Grants to finance construction (*VAIDI*): For 1957–1972, from same source as *GSLIH* above; for 1952–1957, from various issues of *Budget of the United States Government,* Special Analysis D.

Grants to finance highway construction (*VAIDIH*): Same source as *VAIDI*.

Grants to finance "other" construction (*VAIDIO*): Since grants for education construction were small over most of the period, this was derived as *VAIDI* less *VAIDIH*.

Average earnings per full-time state-local employee, education (*WE*): From Table 6.5, *Survey of Current Business.*

Average earnings per full-time, state-local employee, noneducation (*WO*): Same source as *WE*.

Personal income per capita (*Y/N*): *Survey of Current Business,* July 1973, Table 7.6.

# 3

# CHARACTERISTICS OF STATE AND LOCAL TRUST FUNDS

*James A. Maxwell*

This chapter describes the various methods of financing pension funds and provides a thumbnail sketch of the financial characteristics of state and local retirement systems. This is background information for the model of pension fund financing and the forecasts of future fiscal pressure of retirement systems on state and local governments presented in Chapter 4.

Since receipts and expenditures of state and local trust funds are virtually all for retirement plans,[1] the chapter deals solely with retirement plan funds. The first section deals with the methods of financing state and local government pension funds and the sections thereafter with the features of these funds and their recent performance.

## Methods of Financing State and Local Government Employee Retirement Systems

In Holland's terminology, a public arrangement for a pension fund means one "sponsored by government but not designed solely or primarily for that government's employees."[2] The Old Age Survivors and Disability Insurance System (OASDI), the prime example, covers most of the civilian labor force. It operates essentially on a pay-as-you-go basis, with only a small trust fund. This fund is not regarded as a major source of earnings, or as a source from which substantial

[1] In 1972, state and local trust funds made benefit payments of $5,417 million of which $5,000 million was from pension funds. The other $417 million was for cash sickness compensation, which is provided in five states. Data are from U.S. Department of Commerce, Bureau of Economic Analysis, *Survey of Current Business*, July 1973, p. 33.

[2] Daniel M. Holland, *Private Pension Funds: Projected Growth* (New York: National Bureau of Economic Research, 1966), p. 126.

payments will ever be made to retirees. In 1970–1971 receipts and payments of OASDI were, respectively, $31,710 million and $31,101 million, and assets amounting to $34,331 million were only slightly in excess of payments for one year. State and local plans, together with private pension plans, are nonpublic. They are "for the benefit of employees; the trust fund is set up by the employer, but is segregated from his 'business' assets and administered by trustees; the fund is designed to be able to support the pension promises that the plans are making."[3] As a result they accumulate substantial reserves. The reserves of state and local plans at the end of fiscal 1972 amounted to $68,760 million, fourteen times the total annual payments made to beneficiaries by these funds.[4]

Under OASDI the benefits to retirees come chiefly out of payroll tax receipts, supplemented by earnings of a modest reserve fund which is (approximately) equal in amount to annual benefit payments. The payroll tax receipts come from current earnings of covered workers, while the current benefits go to retired workers. Workers provide the benefits received by eligible nonworkers. "The future benefits of present workers, their dependents, or their dependent survivors will be paid in similar fashion out of the contribution of the working population at some future date."[5] So long as population growth and economic growth take place, benefit payments—even increased benefit payments—can be paid from current tax collections without an increase in rates.

In contrast with this (approximate) pay-as-you-go system, most private and state and local government pension plans are funded, at least to some degree, on an actuarial basis. Contribution rates are set at a level so that current receipts exceed current payments. Reserves are accumulated which, when invested, will yield income. (Contributions are made on behalf of each covered worker, generally both by employers and by employees under state and local government plans, but sometimes by the employer alone.) The plan is fully funded—that is, if it were to be closed out at any time, a sufficient reserve fund would have been accumulated to meet all obligations for

---

[3] Ibid., p. 127.

[4] Since details of state and local government pension plans are only available from the Census Bureau, all data references in the chapter are to Bureau of the Census, *Employee-Retirement Systems of State and Local Governments*, vol. 6, no. 1 (1972).

[5] Joseph A. Pechman, Henry J. Aaron, Michael K. Taussig, *Social Security: Perspectives for Reform* (Washington: The Brookings Institution, 1968), p. 71.

all benefits accrued under the plan from its beginning to its end.[6] Partially funded plans—and many state and local government plans fall into this category—do not set aside the contributions required of the employer to meet the above test for full funding.

A few generalizations should be kept in mind on the operation of pension plans over time. A state or local government plan which starts out on a pay-as-you-go basis and continues in this way will, if its membership is normal in its age distribution, have a low level of costs in the early years because it will have a low level of benefit payments to provide for its few retirees. However, as the years pass, and more and more members retire, the level of payments will rise steadily, and so must the level of receipts required from contributors. But after twenty to forty years (the precise time depending chiefly on the age distribution of the membership) the aggregate level of payments and receipts will stabilize, and a static equilibrium will be established.

This static equilibrium is, however, seldom achieved. Rates of compensation, payrolls, the level of benefit payments, the size and composition of the work force—all or some of these will change in unexpected fashion, some increasing and some decreasing the required level of payments and receipts.

On the other hand, if a state or local government system starts out on a fully funded basis and stays on this basis, it will set payments by members so that aggregate receipts at the outset exceed payments, the surplus being invested. If the static equilibrium of such a fund is reached, the level of contributions required will be less than that of a pay-as-you-go system because these receipts will be supplemented by the annual earnings from investments. However, here again unanticipated changes may prevent an equilibrium, and if, as often happens, liberalizing forces gain ascendance, an increased level of contributions will be needed to keep the system fully funded.

The major economic differences between a pay-as-you-go and a fully funded system are that (1) the fully funded system provides for saving and investment and (2) the fully funded system is based on *quid pro quo* finance. An employee of a fully funded system who contributes during his working years to a retirement system, and whose employer also makes a contribution as deferred compensation due to him, gets back on retirement the aggregate of these contributions plus their accumulated earnings. The retirement benefits of an employee of a pay-as-you-go system, on the other hand, will come,

[6] See W. C. Greenough and F. P. King, *Retirement and Insurance Plans in American Colleges* (New York: Columbia University Press, 1959), pp. 89-90.

in large part, from contributions of those who are currently at work; it is not *quid pro quo*.[7]

Even when state and local retirement systems start on a funded basis, they often have difficulty in maintaining full funding. The recent great expansion of state and local government employment has brought collective bargaining between these governments and their workers over wages, and especially over fringe benefits, including pensions. Pension benefits can be liberalized without an immediate increase in current costs, and the political process is susceptible to increases of this sort because the conduct of state and local politicians is often "determined by relatively short-run considerations. The impact of failing to adhere to actuarial principles will frequently fall upon a different mayor and a different city council. In these circumstances, concessions that condemn a city to future impoverishment may not seem intolerable." [8] The Permanent Commission on Public Employee Pensions and Retirement Systems of the State of New York, aware of this bias, recommended in July 1973 that public pensions not be subject to collective negotiations.[9] When a pension scheme, because of liberalization, becomes burdensome to the finances of a state or local government, it is seldom possible to abridge the rights of persons already in the system, inasmuch as the benefit provisions create a contract, and many state constitutions prohibit abridgement of contracts. In such cases, relief can come only through the provision of lower pensions for new entrants.

The policy situation is, therefore, paradoxical. A state or local government cannot count on continued expansion of its population and its economic base. It would be sensible for a state or local government retirement system to acknowledge and provide for the costs of future benefits when the promise of future benefits is made. This would require the accumulation of assets to meet future liabilities. Unfortunately, the political processes are not geared to a disci-

[7] Richard A. Musgrave describes a system of old-age insurance in which benefits and contributions are *quid pro quo* as follows: "Those of working age when the plan is introduced can be called upon to contribute the full amount of their future benefit, adjusted to an actuarial basis and discounted to its present value in the initial period. As the system matures, the contributions of those of working age, together with the capital income of the reserve account, will pay the benefits of the aged. Throughout, the principle of intergeneration equity is complied with." Musgrave, *Theory of Public Finance* (New York: McGraw-Hill, 1959), p. 566. It is an irony of language that he calls this a "pay-as-you-go basis."

[8] H. H. Wellington and Ralph K. Winter, Jr., *The Unions and the Cities* (Washington: The Brookings Institution, 1971), pp. 19-20.

[9] State of New York, Executive Department, *Report of the Permanent Commission on Public Employee Pension and Retirement Systems* (known as the "Kinzel Report"), January 30, 1973, p. 21.

pline of this sort, and the temptation to break the rules by failing to provide receipts in excess of current disbursements is omnipresent.

### Special Features of State and Local Systems

State and local government systems, while similar in structure to private systems, have nonetheless developed important differences from the purely private funds. Overall, the state and local government pension systems provide more generous benefits than do private systems. The normal retirement age and service requirements are more generous than those of private plans, and they are more likely to have generous disability and survivor coverage. Most state and local government pensions are based on final average pay, whereas private pensions are often based on a flat dollar amount graded according to length of service for hourly rated employees, and on career average earnings for salaried employees. Most state and local government systems require employee contributions, whereas most private plans do not.

At one time the relative generosity of state and local pension plans was regarded as an offset for the low earnings of state and local government employees compared to that earned in similar jobs elsewhere. Although the disparity between state and local government earnings and private earnings has narrowed or vanished in recent years, the benefit bias not only remains but has accelerated in the last decade. Because the services of city governments are labor-intensive, the recent expansion in city services has brought a rapid increase in employment and payrolls. State and local government employment grew from 5,548 million persons in 1957 to 10,934 million in 1972, an annual rate of increase of 4.6 percent.[10] Over the same period, private employment grew at a 1.6 percent annual rate, while employment at the federal level grew only 1.3 percent a year.[11] This growth, coupled with the growth of union organization, brought an upsurge in personnel costs, as well as a marked extension of fringe benefits—shorter workweeks, longer vacations, extra holidays, more generous sick leave, and earlier retirement with fewer years of service.

[10] Data are for average number of full and part-time employees during the calendar year; data for 1957 are from U.S. Department of Commerce, Bureau of Economic Analysis, *The National Income and Product Accounts of the United States, 1929-1965* (Washington: U.S. Government Printing Office, 1966), p. 101. Data for 1972 are from U.S. Department of Commerce, *Survey of Current Business*, July 1973, p. 41.

[11] U.S. Department of Commerce, *Survey of Current Business*, July 1973, p. 41.

The last of these has the short-run attraction of being less costly in the early than in the later years. Representative Martha Griffiths has pointed out the effects:

> Suppose you permit local employees to retire after 20 years on half pay, one could then be in the position of supporting two employees, in effect, for every one that was working, assuming a 40-year work life. Thus, you would be paying out the equivalent of two full employees salaries for each job performed. This would virtually double payroll within a measurable period of years.[12]

The Advisory Commission on Intergovernmental Relations has observed that "improvements in pension benefits have particularly insidious effects on city cost levels because these improvements can be passed forward many years into the future. There is evidence to indicate that this is occurring in many cities." [13]

The likelihood is that the financing of retirement systems will be a serious problem for many state and local governments in the next decade. Those that are funded will have to generate larger and larger surpluses to provide the reserves necessary to maintain the funding for the enriched benefits. Those plans that tend more to a pay-as-you-go basis of financing will find the state-local contributions rising sharply later on, as the promises come due. To ascertain how serious this problem may be, it is necessary to discuss the salient characteristics of state and local government pension plans.

## Characteristics of State and Local Systems

**Growth.** The earliest state and local government retirement systems resembled insurance policies limited to special groups of employees (policemen, firemen, teachers) with benefits paid only in the event of death or disability. Coverage of general employees of the state government started in 1911 in Massachusetts. Thereafter, growth was steady, and by the 1940s about one-half of all state and local governments had some form of retirement coverage. Table 3–1 shows recent membership in state and local systems in relation to the number of

---

[12] *Tax Foundation Review*, January 1972, p. 4.

[13] *City Financial Emergencies: The Intergovernmental Dimension* (Washington, D. C., 1973), p. 33. The small city of Hamtramck, Michigan was an extreme case. Police and fireman requirements for current pension payrolls totalled 22 percent of its 1972 budget. The city charter was amended so that new police and firemen coming on the force did not receive the high benefits provided to police and firemen already on the force.

## Table 3–1

FULL-TIME STATE AND LOCAL GOVERNMENT EMPLOYEES AND CURRENT CONTRIBUTORS TO STATE AND LOCAL RETIREMENT SYSTEMS, 1957–1972

(persons in thousands)

| | **1957** (April) | **1962** (October) | **1967** (October) | **1972** (October) |
|---|---|---|---|---|
| Full-time employees | 4,593 | 5,669 | 7,055 | 8,533 |
| Current contributors[a] | 3,729 | 4,961 | 6,465 | 8,407 |
| Percent covered | 81.2 | 87.5 | 91.6 | 98.5 |

[a] End of fiscal year.

**Source:** Bureau of the Census, *Employer-Retirement Systems of State and Local Governments,* vol. 4, no. 1 (1957); vol. 6, no. 1 (1962); vol. 6, no. 2 (1967); vol. 6, no. 1 (1972). (This reference is also the source of Figure 3-1 and Tables 3-3 through 3-25.) Bureau of the Census, *Compendium of Public Employment,* vol. 3, no. 2 (1967); and vol. 3, no. 2 (1972).

full-time state and local government employees.[14] The increase in state and local government employment since 1957 has been at the rate of 4.5 percent a year.[15] The increase, as Table 3–2 shows, was five times as fast as the federal increase in civilian employment, and nearly three times as fast as total civilian employment. Pension coverage is virtually universal for full-time employees—over 98 percent are current contributors. In 1966 Daniel Holland estimated that employment by state and local governments would continue to grow faster than total employment, perhaps at a rate of 4.7 percent.[16] So far this estimate has been quite accurate, but some slowdown seems likely for the years from 1973 to 1981.

[14] Beginning in 1951, and especially since 1954, coverage in OASDI has been available to most state and local employees. "Of the 4.8 million state and local government employees covered under the Social Security Act in January 1965, 3.5 million were also members of staff retirement systems—that is, they had dual coverage." Social Security Administration, *State and Local Retirement Systems,* Office of Research and Statistics, Research Report No. 15, 1965, p. 2. In 1967 seven states did not allow their employees to be members of social security. The "Kinzel Report" (State of New York, Executive Department, *Report of the Permanent Commission on Public Employee Pension and Retirement Systems,* January 30, 1973), argued that states should shape their own systems so they would be integrated and consistent with the federal system.

[15] The slight differences between this figure and the one cited previously is the result of differences in data sources. The data here are Bureau of Census figures as of October each year; the previous data are from the Commerce Department and are for average annual employment.

[16] Holland, *Private Pension Funds,* p. 126.

## Table 3–2

PUBLIC AND CIVILIAN EMPLOYMENT, 1957–1972

(persons in thousands)

| | State and Local Government[a] | Federal Government | Civilian |
|---|---|---|---|
| 1957 | 5,608 | 2,439 | 64,071 |
| 1962 | 6,849 | 2,539 | 66,702 |
| 1967 | 8,874 | 2,993 | 74,372 |
| 1972 | 10,808 | 2,795 | 81,702 |
| Annual rate of increase, 1957–1972 | 4.5% | 0.9% | 1.6% |

[a] These figures are for full-time and part-time employees in October.

**Source:** *1967 Census of Governments, Topical Studies,* no. 5, p. 61; *Public Employment in 1972,* p. 7.

## Table 3–3

NUMBER AND MEMBERSHIP OF STATE AND LOCALLY ADMINISTERED RETIREMENT SYSTEMS, 1957–1972

| Item | 1957 | 1967 | 1972 |
|---|---|---|---|
| Number of systems | | | |
| State-administered | 147 | 183 | 176 |
| Locally administered | 2,058 | 1,982 | 2,128 |
| Total | 2,205 | 2,165 | 2,304 |
| Membership (in thousands) | | | |
| State-administered | 3,036 | 5,786 | 7,506 |
| Locally administered | 985 | 1,238 | 1,582 |
| Total | 4,021 | 7,069 | 9,088 |
| Membership (in percent) | | | |
| State-administered | 76 | 82 | 83 |
| Locally administered | 24 | 18 | 17 |
| Total | 100 | 100 | 100 |

**Membership.** State and local government systems are split into state-administered and locally administered. In 1972 state-administered systems numbered 176 and locally administered systems 2,128—a total of 2,304 systems (Table 3–3). Many state-administered plans cover employees of local governments as well as of state governments. Membership in state-administered systems is growing faster than membership in locally administered plans. In 1972 the membership in state-administered systems was 83 percent of total membership, and their average membership per system was 42,649, compared to 748 for local systems. Although the swing to larger units is evident, small units are numerous (as Table 3–4 shows), especially among the locally administered systems. In 1972 nearly 91 percent of these locally administered systems had a membership of less than 1,000. At the other end of the scale, the 110 systems with a membership of 10,000 or more contained over 90 percent of the total membership of state and local government systems.

**Coverage Classes.** The two broad categories of plans are those of "general" and those of "limited" coverage, of which the former (general coverage) had 59 percent of total membership in 1972 (Table 3–5). Teachers and other school employees dominate the limited coverage category.

**Beneficiaries.** Table 3–6 shows the number of beneficiaries of the state and local government pension systems, divided into normal retirement beneficiaries, disability beneficiaries, and survivors. In 1972 beneficiaries totalled 1,463,400, approximately 16.1 percent of the membership. The ratio of beneficiaries to total membership has crept up from 13.0 percent in 1957 to 16.1 percent in 1972. The increase in the ratio accelerated during the years from 1967 to 1972 and was concentrated

**Table 3–4**

MEMBERSHIP SIZE OF STATE AND LOCAL RETIREMENT SYSTEMS, 1972

| Membership | Total | State-Administered | Locally Administered |
|---|---|---|---|
| Less than 100 | 1,437 | 27 | 1,480 |
| 100–199 | 248 | 11 | 237 |
| 200–499 | 183 | 11 | 172 |
| 500–999 | 126 | 13 | 113 |
| 1,000–4,999 | 153 | 18 | 135 |
| 5,000–9,999 | 47 | 9 | 38 |
| 10,000 or more | 110 | 87 | 23 |
| Total | 2,304 | 176 | 2,128 |

**Table 3–5**

DISTRIBUTION OF MEMBERSHIP OF STATE AND LOCAL RETIREMENT SYSTEMS, 1967 AND 1972

| | 1967 | 1972 |
|---|---|---|
| General coverage | 56.9% | 58.9% |
| Limited coverage | 43.1 | 41.1 |
| Teachers and other school employees | 37.3 | 35.3 |
| Police and firemen | 3.7 | 3.5 |
| Other | 2.1 | 2.3 |

**Table 3–6**

NUMBER OF BENEFICIARIES AND RATIO OF BENEFICIARIES TO MEMBERSHIP IN STATE AND LOCAL RETIREMENT SYSTEMS, 1957–1972

| Item | 1957 | 1962 | 1967 | 1972 |
|---|---|---|---|---|
| Number of beneficiaries (in thousands) | | | | |
| Normal retirement | 424.2 | 600.2 | 844.5 | 1,241.0 |
| Disability | 43.4 | 60.7 | 77.2 | 92.4 |
| Survivors | 54.8 | 78.1 | 108.2 | 130.1 |
| Total | 522.4 | 739.0 | 1,029.0 | 1,463.4 |
| Ratio of beneficiaries to membership (percent) | | | | |
| All systems | 13.0 | 13.8 | 14.6 | 16.1 |
| State-administered | 9.4 | 10.5 | 11.7 | 13.9 |
| Locally administered | 24.2 | 26.3 | 27.4 | 26.7 |

in the state-administered systems. The overall ratio of beneficiaries to contributors is twice as high for locally administered systems as for state-administered plans. It may be noted that there is variation in this ratio from state to state (Table 3–7), especially among the local systems. The locally administered systems of eighteen states in 1972 had beneficiary/contributor ratios which exceeded 30 percent, and the drift of these systems toward even higher ratios was significant during the years from 1967 to 1972.

## Table 3–7

DISTRIBUTION BY STATE OF RATIOS OF BENEFICIARIES TO MEMBERSHIP, 1967 AND 1972

| Ratios | State-Administered (number of states) | | Locally Administered (number of states) | |
|---|---|---|---|---|
| | 1967 | 1972 | 1967 | 1972 |
| 0.0– 4.9 | 2 | — | — | — |
| 5.0– 9.9 | 18 | 111 | 2 | 1 |
| 10.0–14.9 | 17 | 17 | 2 | 5 |
| 15.0–19.9 | 11 | 16 | 10 | 7 |
| 20.0–24.9 | 1 | 4 | 4 | 8 |
| 25.0–29.9 | — | 1 | 7 | 9 |
| 30.0 and over | 1[a] | 1[a] | 16 | 18 |
| Total | 50 | 50 | 41[b] | 48[b] |

[a] In 1967 the Delaware ratio was 52.8 percent, and in 1972, it was 42.3 percent.
[b] In 1967 nine states, in 1972 two states, had no locally administered systems.

Variation in the ratio of beneficiaries to membership among cities is shown in Table 3–8.

**Receipts.** Revenues of state and local retirement systems come from three sources: (1) employee contributions, (2) government (employer) contributions, and (3) earnings on investments. Total receipts have grown at an annual rate of 11.6 percent between 1957 and 1972 (Table 3–9). Of the three components, by far the fastest growth was in earnings on investments—a rate of 16.4 percent per year over the period from 1957 to 1972. The relative share provided by earnings doubled in this same period: it was 14 percent of total receipts in 1957 and 28 percent in 1972. The relative share provided by government contributions declined slightly and that by employees declined significantly.

As usual, the variation from state to state was striking. In 1972, the governmental contribution of six states and the District of Columbia provided more than half the total revenues of these retirement systems, and in one—Delaware—it provided 87.7 percent. The governmental contribution of the locally administered systems of seven states and the District of Columbia was over 70 percent of total receipts.[17]

[17] The states and percentages were Delaware 85.4, Idaho 70.9, Indiana 89.0, Louisiana 78.0, Mississippi 75.7, New Jersey 71.8, and the District of Columbia 70.5.

**Table 3–8**

MEMBERSHIP AND BENEFICIARIES IN SELECTED LOCAL RETIREMENT SYSTEMS, 1972

(persons in thousands)

| | Membership | Number of Beneficiaries | Ratio |
|---|---|---|---|
| Detroit | | | |
| Police and firemen | 7,330 | 4,237 | 57.8% |
| Minneapolis | | | |
| Police | 800 | 596 | 74.6 |
| Firemen | 516 | 531 | 97.2 |
| St. Paul | | | |
| Police | 530 | 344 | 64.9 |
| Firemen | 463 | 305 | 65.9 |
| St. Louis (Mo.) | | | |
| Police | 2,363 | 983 | 41.6 |
| Firemen | 1,500 | 900 | 60.0 |
| Milwaukee | | | |
| Police | 209 | 1,104 | 335.8 |
| Firemen | 212 | 712 | 96.0 |
| Wilmington (Del.) | | | |
| Police | 273 | 262 | 90.1 |
| Firemen | 235 | 291 | 123.8 |
| District of Columbia | | | |
| Police | 5,300 | 4,485 | 84.6 |
| Firemen | 6,112 | 2,189 | 35.8 |

The most common method of employee contribution is a specified single percent of salary, although variable percents are also used. The average annual employee contribution in 1972 was $374, with the range running from a low of $243 in Mississippi to a high of $923 in Hawaii.

Examination of receipts in relation to membership (Table 3–10) shows that over the period from 1957 to 1972 the governmental contribution was larger and grew faster than that of employees. In 1972 over half the total revenue of state-administered systems was provided by the governmental contribution in seven states, and more than half the revenue of the locally administered systems was provided by the governmental contribution in thirty-one states and the District of

### Table 3–9

REVENUES OF STATE AND LOCAL RETIREMENT SYSTEMS, 1957–1972

| Item | 1957 | 1962 | 1967 | 1972 | Annual Rate of Increase, 1957–1972 |
|---|---|---|---|---|---|
| | Millions of dollars | | | | |
| Contributions | | | | | |
| Employee | 899 | 1,288 | 1,960 | 3,400 | 9.3% |
| Government | 1,200 | 1,883 | 3,055 | 5,750 | 11.0% |
| Earnings on investments | 357 | 827 | 1,565 | 3,471 | 16.4% |
| Total | 2,455 | 3,997 | 6,580 | 12,621 | 11.6% |
| | Percentage distribution | | | | |
| Contributions | | | | | |
| Employee | 37 | 32 | 30 | 27 | — |
| Government | 49 | 47 | 46 | 45 | — |
| Earnings on investments | 14 | 21 | 24 | 28 | — |
| Total | 100 | 100 | 100 | 100 | — |

### Table 3–10

GOVERNMENT AND EMPLOYEE CONTRIBUTIONS PER MEMBER TO STATE-ADMINISTERED AND LOCALLY ADMINISTERED RETIREMENT SYSTEMS, 1957–1972

| | 1957 | 1967 | 1972 |
|---|---|---|---|
| Dollars | | | |
| Government contribution | 298 | 430 | 632 |
| Employee contribution | 223 | 276 | 374 |
| Index numbers (1957 = 100) | | | |
| Government contribution | 100 | 144 | 212 |
| Employee contribution | 100 | 124 | 167 |

Columbia (Table 3–11). Whereas the governmental contribution per member was more than twice as large in 1972 as it was in 1957, the per-member contribution had grown only by two-thirds (Table 3–10). The lower rate of growth of the employee contribution arises because

**Table 3–11**

GOVERNMENT CONTRIBUTIONS BY STATES AS PERCENT OF REVENUES OF STATE AND LOCAL GOVERNMENT RETIREMENT SYSTEMS, 1972

| Government Contributions (percent) | State-Administered (number of states) | Locally Administered (number of states) |
|---|---|---|
| 20.0–29.9 | 2 | — |
| 30.0–39.9 | 23 | 2 |
| 40.0–49.9 | 19 | 15 |
| 50.0–59.9 | 4 | 19 |
| 60.0–69.9 | 1 | 5 |
| 70.0–79.9 | — | 7[a] |
| 80.0–89.9 | 1 | 1 |
| 90.0–99.9 | 1 | — |
| Total | 50 | 48 |
| Average | 45.6% | 51.8% |

[a] Includes District of Columbia where government contributions amounted to 70.5 percent of revenues.

the percentage rate of contribution has been regarded as a contract not subject to negotiation. Contributions will, of course, grow with expansion of the salary base, but not otherwise.

It may be asked what was the source of the growth in "earnings." The growth was in fact attributable to a growth in assets from $12.8 billion in 1957 to $68.8 billion in 1972 and to a growth in the average rate of earnings (rate of return) from 2.78 percent to 5.05 percent (Table 3–12). Nearly half the earnings growth from 1957 to 1972 was the result of a higher rate of return on assets. If the rate should flatten (or possibly decline) in the years ahead, the future provision for payments to beneficiaries will fall more heavily on government contributions, and this will place heavy budget demands on state and local governments.

The governmental contribution during the years from 1957 to 1972 was substantial. As Table 3–13 shows, payments by state and local governments to their retirement funds have grown faster than general state and local government expenditure. Moreover, the annual rate of increase of contributions by five-year periods has been accelerating: it was 10.1 percent per year from 1962 to 1967, and 13.5 per-

### Table 3–12

ASSETS AND EARNINGS OF STATE AND LOCAL RETIREMENT SYSTEMS, 1957–1972

| Year | Book Value of Assets | Earnings | Average Rate of Return Earnings/Assets (percent) |
|---|---|---|---|
| | In millions of dollars | | |
| 1957 | 12,834 | 357 | 2.78 |
| 1967 | 39,765 | 1,565 | 3.99 |
| 1972 | 68,760 | 3,471 | 5.05 |
| | Relative numbers (1957 = 100) | | |
| 1957 | 100 | 100 | 100 |
| 1967 | 306 | 438 | 144 |
| 1972 | 538 | 972 | 182 |

### Table 3–13

STATE AND LOCAL GOVERNMENT GENERAL EXPENDITURES AND CONTRIBUTIONS TO RETIREMENT SYSTEMS, 1957–1972

| Year | Contributions | General Expenditure | General Expenditure Less Intergovernmental |
|---|---|---|---|
| | In millions of dollars | | |
| 1957 | 1,200 | 40,375 | 36,532 |
| 1962 | 1,883 | 59,713 | 48,601 |
| 1967 | 3,055 | 93,350 | 77,980 |
| 1972 | 5,750 | 166,873 | 129,543 |
| | Annual rates of increase (percent) | | |
| 1957–62 | 11.0 | 9.9 | 8.8 |
| 1962–67 | 10.1 | 9.3 | 9.9 |
| 1967–72 | 13.5 | 12.3 | 10.8 |

cent per year for 1967–1972. The growth of general expenditure in the fifteen years, 1957–1972, has itself been remarkable—a rate of 9.9 percent per year. Since the growth in general expenditures is in part attributable to the growth of intergovernmental expenditure (which is included in the general expenditure of the government making the final disbursement), and since state and local contributions

**Table 3–14**

PAYMENTS BY STATE AND LOCAL GOVERNMENT RETIREMENT SYSTEMS, 1957–1972

| | Payments ($ millions) | Benefits ($ millions) | Withdrawal ($ millions) | Other ($ millions) | Monthly Payment Per Beneficiary |
|---|---|---|---|---|---|
| 1957 | 958 | 725 | 216 | 17 | 116 |
| 1962 | 1,589 | 1,259 | 308 | 22 | 137 |
| 1967 | 2,648 | 2,103 | 506 | 75 | 162 |
| 1972 | 4,920 | 4,121 | 647 | 152 | 223 |
| Annual rate of increase | 11.5% | 12.3% | 7.6% | 15.7% | 4.5% |

to their retirement funds do not receive federal aid, a better comparison would be between state and local contributions to retirement funds and general expenditure less intergovernmental aid.[18] The figures for this comparison are also given in Table 3–13. The rate of growth of contributions greatly exceeded that of general expenditure out of own resources. For the period as a whole, contributions grew at an annual rate of 11 percent, while expenditures from own resources grew at 8.8 percent per annum.

**Payments.** Table 3–14 shows that payments by state and local government retirement funds increased from $958 million to $4,920 million in the period from 1957 to 1972, an annual rate of increase of 11.5 percent. The monthly payment per beneficiary grew much more slowly—at a 4.5 percent rate—which means that most of the increase in payments came from an increase in the number of beneficiaries. Nonetheless, payments per beneficiary grew by 38 percent in the five years from 1967 to 1972, and this is more than double the percentage increase for the two previous five-year periods. It seems certain that the rate of growth of payments per beneficiary will accelerate in the years to come through liberalization of benefit provisions and in response to inflation. In addition, the number of beneficiaries can be expected to grow faster than the numbers of contributors as the systems mature.

Payments per beneficiary are usually larger in limited than in general coverage systems: in 1972 the averages were $276 and $179.

[18] Census reports on government finances regard contributions to employee retirement funds as intergovernmental transactions. They are netted out to avoid duplication.

Moreover, "beneficiaries with dual coverages (OASDI as well as state and local) generally enjoyed a higher retirement income than those covered only by a state or local pension system."[19] As always, great variation exists from state to state. Average monthly benefits in 1972 ranged from $63 and $43 in Iowa and South Dakota to $300 and $385 in New York and Delaware. (The District of Columbia figure was $547.)

The methods used to determine eligibility for benefits are diverse. For normal retirement (not disability) the Tax Foundation study reported that in 1965–1966 "half the systems representing about two-fifths of the membership based retirement *eligibility* on an age requirement. . . . The largest proportion of membership—58 percent—belonged to systems which based retirement eligibility on a combination of age and some minimum of service."[20]

Formulas used to determine the amount of the benefit to which an eligible retiree may be entitled are of two kinds. (1) benefits calculated on the basis of a specified percentage of "final average salary" times each year of service, or (2) benefits based partly on final average salary and partly on the proceeds of an annuity purchased with employee contributions. Final average salary has many definitions, but it is often the salary for some specified period of employment experience (five years or more or less). The percentage or percentages applied are diverse:

> For example, in one particular system the benefits level is computed on the basis of 2 percent of the first $300 monthly salary plus 1.5 percent of salary over $300, all multiplied by the number of years of service. Thus an employee retiring after 25 years with an average (monthly) salary of $450 would compute his benefit as follows: [0.02 ($300) + 0.015 ($150)] × 25 = $206.25.[21]

**Payments in Relation to Receipts.** Table 3–7 shows that the number of beneficiaries grew faster than the number of members from 1957 to 1972. In the period 1957–1967, payments to beneficiaries also grew faster than receipts, the ratio of payments to receipts rising from 39.0 percent in 1957 to 40.8 percent in 1967 (Table 3–15). However, after 1967, receipts spurted ahead, and the ratio fell again to 39.0 percent in 1972. The receipts most responsible for this change were

[19] Tax Foundation, Inc., *State and Local Employee Pension Systems* (New York: Tax Foundation, Inc., 1969), p. 19.

[20] Ibid.

[21] Ibid., p. 23.

**Table 3–15**

RECEIPTS AND PAYMENTS OF STATE AND LOCAL RETIREMENT SYSTEMS, 1957–1972

($ in millions)

| | 1957 | 1962 | 1967 | 1972 |
|---|---|---|---|---|
| All systems | | | | |
| Receipts | 2,455 | 3,997 | 6,580 | 12,620 |
| Payments | 958 | 1,567 | 2,684 | 4,920 |
| Ratio of payments to receipts | 39.0% | 39.2% | 40.8% | 39.0% |
| State-administered | | | | |
| Receipts | 1,504 | 2,695 | 4,656 | 9,285 |
| Payments | 522 | 948 | 1,654 | 3,279 |
| Ratio of payments to receipts | 34.7% | 35.2% | 35.5% | 35.3% |
| Locally administered | | | | |
| Receipts | 951 | 1,302 | 1,924 | 3,335 |
| Payments | 437 | 641 | 1,030 | 1,641 |
| Ratio of payments to receipts | 46.0% | 49.2% | 53.5% | 49.2% |

earnings on investments, which grew from $1,565 million in 1967 to $3,471 million in 1972. Thus, if the rate of growth of earnings is not maintained in the future, the rise in the ratio of payments to receipts will be resumed. The average payments/receipts ratio for locally administered funds is larger than that for state-administered funds—49.2 percent compared with 35.3 percent in 1972. Locally administered funds are often older and more mature than state-administered funds. Moreover, variation in their ratios from state to state (Table 3–16) is greater than the variation for state-administered funds.

Examination of the locally administered systems of the twenty-nine largest cities (Table 3–17) shows that many of them are in trouble.[22] The range of payment/receipts ratios runs from 15.1 percent and 18.2 percent for Phoenix and San Jose to 100.6 percent and 101.7 percent for Indianapolis and Pittsburgh. Thirteen of the cities have ratios over 50 percent [23] and nine of them showed a population

[22] Three large cities are not included. Cleveland and Honolulu were excluded because their systems are state-administered, and Buffalo because figures are not available.

[23] No relationship to size of the cities is evident.

## Table 3–16

DISTRIBUTION BY STATES OF THE RATIOS OF PAYMENTS TO RECEIPTS OF STATE-ADMINISTERED AND LOCALLY ADMINISTERED RETIREMENT SYSTEMS, 1957–1972

| | Total | | | State-Administered | | | Locally Administered | | |
|---|---|---|---|---|---|---|---|---|---|
| **Ratios** | 1957 | 1967 | 1972 | 1957 | 1967 | 1972 | 1957 | 1967 | 1972 |
| 0.0– 9.9 | — | — | — | — | — | — | — | 1 | — |
| 10.0–19.9 | 1 | 1 | 2 | 6 | 3 | 2 | — | 1 | 2 |
| 20.0–29.9 | 13 | 8 | 9 | 11 | 16 | 13 | 1 | 1 | 4 |
| 30.0–39.9 | 15 | 22 | 24 | 15 | 15 | 23 | 9 | 7 | 12 |
| 40.0–49.9 | 5 | 10 | 8 | 8 | 8 | 5 | 4 | 12 | 7 |
| 50.0–59.9 | 10 | 6 | 3 | 4 | 4 | 3 | 10 | 10 | 6 |
| 60.0–69.9 | 3 | 2 | 2 | 2 | 3 | 2 | 8 | 3 | 9 |
| 70.0–79.9 | 2 | — | 1 | — | — | 1 | 4 | 4 | 4 |
| 80.0–89.9 | 2 | 2 | 2 | 1 | — | — | 1 | 4 | 3 |
| 90.0–99.9 | — | — | — | — | — | — | 2 | 1 | 2 |
| 100 or more | — | — | — | 1 | 1 | 1 | 2[a] | 5[a] | — |
| Total | 51 | 51 | 51 | 48 | 50 | 50 | 41 | 49 | 49 |

[a] In 1957 the ratios for Missouri and Indiana were, respectively, 100 and 160; in 1967 the ratios were 154 for Maine, 108 for Mississippi, 103 for New Jersey, 116 for Utah, and 122 for Wyoming.

## Table 3–17

RATIOS OF PAYMENTS TO RECEIPTS OF LOCALLY ADMINISTERED RETIREMENT SYSTEMS OF THE TWENTY-NINE LARGEST CITIES, 1972

| City | Ratio | City | Ratio |
|---|---|---|---|
| Phoenix | 15.1 | Chicago | 48.7 |
| San Jose | 18.2 | Atlanta | 54.0 |
| Kansas City | 20.0 | New York | 54.4 |
| Dallas | 23.8 | Minneapolis | 56.6 |
| Houston | 26.2 | Seattle | 60.2 |
| San Antonio | 28.6 | Philadelphia | 61.7 |
| Baltimore | 28.8 | Nashville | 71.4 |
| Cincinnati | 29.7 | New Orleans | 75.2 |
| St. Louis | 32.0 | Boston | 76.5 |
| San Diego | 36.8 | Jacksonville | 80.2 |
| Detroit | 37.4 | Denver[a] | 80.4 |
| Memphis | 37.6 | District of Columbia | 87.5 |
| Milwaukee | 38.5 | Indianapolis | 100.6 |
| San Francisco | 39.6 | Pittsburgh | 101.7 |
| Los Angeles | 41.0 | | |

[a] This figure is only for the limited coverage systems.

decline in the decade from 1960 to 1970. At the other end of the scale, the six cities with the lowest ratios in 1972 all showed a population increase in this decade.

**Assets.** As Table 3–18 shows, assets of state and local retirement systems grew from $12.8 billion in 1957 to $68.8 billion in 1972. Those of state-administered systems grew faster than those of locally administered systems: they accounted for 62.7 percent of total assets in 1957 and 74.4 percent in 1972. Assets per member grew from $3,191 in 1957 to $7,565 in 1972 (by 137 percent). Locally administered plans have greater assets per member than state-administered plans partly because of the higher salaries of their limited coverage membership, and partly because they have been in existence longer.

The composition of assets changed significantly over the period from 1957 to 1972. As Table 3-19 shows, nongovernmental assets (securities) were 32.8 percent of the total in 1957 and 90.1 percent in 1972, while governmental assets (securities) shrank from 65.6 percent of the portfolio to 8.7 percent. Moreover, the composition of the nongovernmental assets also changed, with a large relative growth

**Table 3–18**

ASSETS OF STATE-ADMINISTERED AND LOCALLY ADMINISTERED RETIREMENT SYSTEMS, 1957–1972

| Item and Administrative Unit | 1957 | 1962 | 1967 | 1972 |
|---|---|---|---|---|
| Total assets ($ billions) | | | | |
| State-administered | 8.0 | 15.5 | 27.7 | 51.2 |
| Locally administered | 4.8 | 7.8 | 11.6 | 17.6 |
| Total | 12.8 | 23.3 | 39.3 | 68.8 |
| Percent distribution of total assets | | | | |
| State-administered | 62.7 | 66.5 | 70.5 | 74.4 |
| Locally administered | 37.3 | 33.5 | 29.5 | 25.6 |
| Total | 100.0 | 100.0 | 100.0 | 100.0 |
| Assets per member (in dollars) | | | | |
| State-administered | 2,651 | 3,653 | 4,782 | 6,815 |
| Locally administered | 4,856 | 6,971 | 9,043 | 11,121 |
| Total | 3,191 | 4,340 | 5,555 | 7,565 |

### Table 3–19
ASSETS OF STATE AND LOCAL RETIREMENT SYSTEMS, 1957–1972

| Type of Asset | 1957 | 1962 | 1967 | 1972 |
|---|---|---|---|---|
| | Billions of dollars | | | |
| Governmental securities | 8.4 | 10.1 | 9.1 | 6.0 |
| Nongovernmental securities | 4.2 | 12.9 | 29.7 | 62.0 |
| Corporate bonds | (3.4) | — | — | (38.1) |
| Corporate stocks | (0.2) | — | — | (12.6) |
| Mortgages | (0.4) | — | — | (7.0) |
| Other | (0.2) | — | — | (4.3) |
| Cash | 0.2 | 0.3 | 0.4 | 0.8 |
| Total | 12.8 | 23.3 | 39.3 | 68.8 |
| | Percentage distribution | | | |
| Governmental securities | 65.6 | 43.3 | 23.2 | 8.7 |
| Nongovernmental securities | 32.8 | 55.4 | 75.6 | 90.1 |
| Corporate bonds | (26.4) | — | — | (55.3) |
| Corporate stocks | (1.4) | — | | (18.3) |
| Mortgages | (3.6) | — | — | (10.2) |
| Other | (1.4) | — | — | (6.3) |
| Cash | 1.6 | 1.3 | 1.2 | 1.2 |
| Total | 100.0 | 100.0 | 100.0 | 100.0 |

in holdings of corporate stocks (although in 1972 stocks were only 20.3 percent of nongovernmental assets and 18.3 percent of total assets). The shift away from holdings of governmental to nongovernmental securities made by the state-administered systems was greater than the shift made by the locally administered plans. In 1972, 75 percent of the assets of state-administered plans were nongovernmental compared with 67 percent for locally administered plans.

The shift in the composition of assets during 1957–1972 was presumably responsible for the growth in the rate of earnings from 2.78 percent (of the book value of assets) in 1957 to 5.05 percent in 1972 (Table 3–12). The rise in the rate of earnings of the state-administered plans was higher than that of locally administered plans —in 1972 5.12 percent compared with 4.83 percent.

**Assets Per Member by States.** Variation among states in the amount of assets per member is notable, ranging in 1972 from $13,408 in Hawaii to $989 in Delaware, with the other states strung out in between. In 1972, when the average assets per member amounted to $7,565, twenty-seven states were below the average (Table 3–20).

**Payments-to-Assets Ratio.** When a system operates more or less on a pay-as-you-go basis, it will build up a low asset level and will, therefore, derive small annual earnings from its assets. Reliance will be placed on receipts from government and working members for the provision of benefits promised to retirees. On the other hand, a system which is fully funded will accumulate substantial assets, the earnings from which will finance a large portion of annual benefit payments. It follows that the ratio of current payments to assets gives a rough indication of the financial strength or weakness of a fund—a high ratio showing weakness and a low ratio showing strength.

Table 3–21 shows that some time in the mid-1960s, the ratio of payments to assets began to rise, particularly in the case of the locally administered funds. Over the five years from 1967 to 1972, the rise in the ratio was significant—from 6.84 percent to 7.16 percent.

When state-by-state ratios are examined (Table 3–22), it appears that in 1972 the systems of a few states were in trouble. The extreme case was Delaware, where payments were nearly twice the amount of assets. Three other states with high payments/assets ratios for the

**Table 3–20**

PER-MEMBER ASSETS OF STATE AND LOCAL RETIREMENT SYSTEMS, 1957–1972

| | Number of States | | |
|---|---|---|---|
| **Assets Per Member** | 1957 | 1967 | 1972 |
| Under $1,000 | 5 | 1 | 1 |
| $1,000–1,999 | 22 | 3 | 1 |
| $2,000–2,999 | 12 | 12 | 4 |
| $3,000–3,999 | 4 | 13 | 8 |
| $4,000–4,999 | 6 | 8 | 9 |
| $5,000–5,999 | — | 6 | 8 |
| $6,000–6,999 | — | 4 | 5 |
| $7,000 or more | 1 | 3 | 14 |
| Total | 50 | 50 | 50 |
| Average per member | $3,191 | $5,555 | $7,565 |

### Table 3–21

RATIOS OF AGGREGATE PAYMENTS TO ASSETS OF STATE-ADMINISTERED AND LOCALLY ADMINISTERED RETIREMENT SYSTEMS, 1957–1972

| | Total | State-Administered | Locally Administered |
|---|---|---|---|
| 1957 | 7.46 | 6.48 | 9.13 |
| 1962 | 6.82 | 6.10 | 8.27 |
| 1967 | 6.84 | 5.98 | 8.88 |
| 1972 | 7.16 | 6.41 | 9.32 |

### Table 3–22

RATIOS OF PAYMENTS TO ASSETS BY STATES OF STATE-ADMINISTERED AND LOCALLY ADMINISTERED RETIREMENT SYSTEMS, 1957–1972

| | Total (number of states) | | State-Administered (number of states) | | Locally Administered (number of states) | |
|---|---|---|---|---|---|---|
| **Ratios** | 1957 | 1972 | 1957 | 1972 | 1957 | 1972 |
| 0.0– 4.9 | 7 | 7 | 15 | 12 | — | 4 |
| 5.0– 9.9 | 26 | 35 | 26 | 30 | 14 | 20 |
| 10.0–14.9 | 16 | 3 | 8 | 4 | 11 | 8 |
| 15.0–19.9 | — | 4 | — | — | 4 | 4 |
| 20.0 and over | 1 | 1 | 1 | 3 | 12 | 11 |
| Total | 50 | 50 | 50 | 49 | 41 | 47 |

state-administered systems were Massachusetts (19.3 percent), West Virginia (18.0 percent), and Maine (16.6 percent). It might appear from the frequencies of the locally administered systems for 1972 (shown in Table 3–22) that several of them were in trouble: in eleven states, payments were 20.0 percent or more of assets. However, only in Nebraska, Pennsylvania, and West Virginia are the figures for locally administered systems significant; in the other eight states the systems are small and/or on their way to extinction.

**Comparison of Payments/Receipts and Payments/Assets Ratios.** Overall, the state-by-state relationship between the ratios of payments to receipts and payments to assets is quite close. When the two sets of ratios are ranked and correlated, the Spearman rank correlation coefficient is +0.83, being closer at both ends of the two series and blurred in the middle (Table 3–23 and Figure 3–1).

## Conclusions

In recent years membership in state and local government retirement systems has expanded more rapidly than the number of state and local employees. In 1972, 98 percent of full-time employees were members of the state and local systems—a figure which must be close to the practical ceiling. Future growth in membership is likely to do no more than keep pace with growth in employment, and the likelihood is that employment will not rise at the pace of the last decade. No less than 2,304 different state and local retirement systems were in operation in 1972. Although they do have a common form and pattern, the variation among them in size and composition of membership, amount of assets, and financial structure of payments and benefits is great. In 1972 the 157 largest systems contained 93 percent of total membership. Nonetheless, small systems persist, and 1,437 of the systems had fewer than 100 members in 1972.

**Table 3–23**

STATES WITH THE HIGHEST AND LOWEST RATIOS OF PAYMENTS TO RECEIPTS AND PAYMENTS TO ASSETS OF STATE-ADMINISTERED AND LOCALLY ADMINISTERED RETIREMENT SYSTEMS, 1972

| | P/R Ratios | Rank | P/A Ratios | Rank |
|---|---|---|---|---|
| Highest | | | | |
| Delaware | 85.2 | 1 | 183.9 | 1 |
| Maine | 77.7 | 2 | 16.6 | 5 |
| West Virginia | 65.9 | 3 | 18.2 | 2 |
| Massachusetts | 63.7 | 4 | 17.6 | 3 |
| Indiana | 58.6 | 5 | 16.7 | 4 |
| Lowest | | | | |
| South Carolina | 23.9 | 46 | 4.0 | 48 |
| North Carolina | 22.7 | 47.5 | 4.0 | 48 |
| Wyoming | 22.7 | 47.5 | 5.0 | 46 |
| Arizona | 19.5 | 49 | 3.4 | 50 |
| Alaska | 13.3 | 50 | 4.0 | 48 |

**Figure 3–1**

STATES RANKED BY RATIOS OF PAYMENTS TO RECEIPTS (P/R) AND OF PAYMENTS TO ASSETS (P/A), 1972

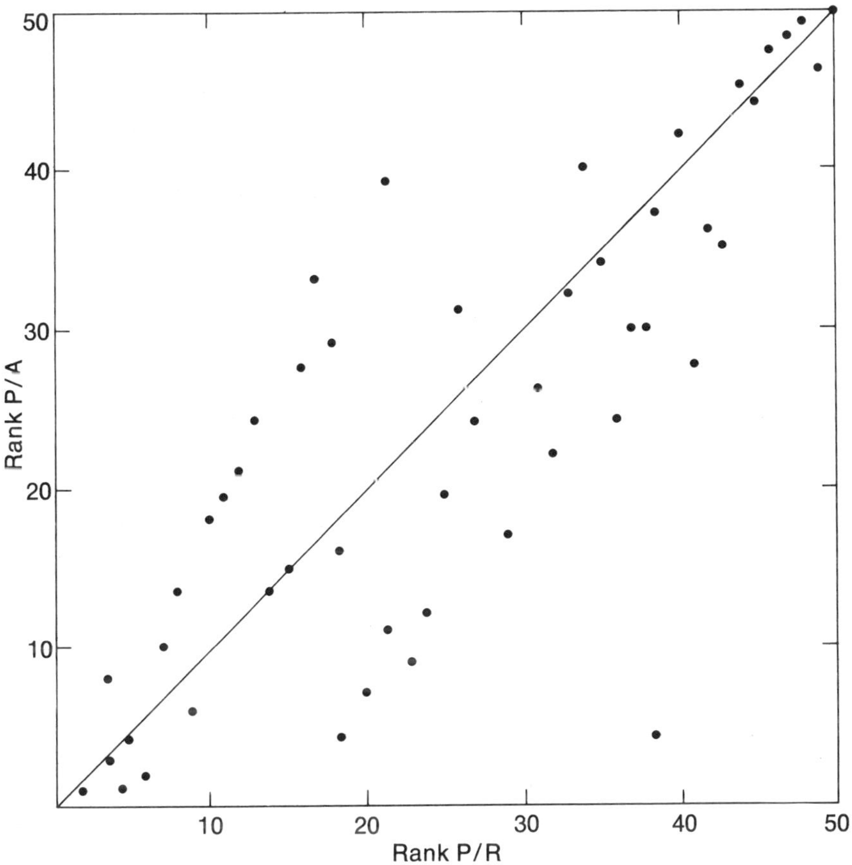


The diversity of the systems means that generalizations on their finances have limited validity. Systems which are new and expanding in membership have few current beneficiaries and a considerable excess of annual receipts over annual payments. Older systems have a relatively large number of beneficiaries and a rising annual ratio of payments to receipts. The diversity is compounded because some systems, even when new, pursue a full-funding policy, while others operate pay-as-you-go, and still others in between.

This diversity means that, over time, trends are obscured. They are further obscured because of the time lag in the impact of most changes in a system. Lowering the retirement age, for example, affects immediately only the annual trickle of members who retire. Higher benefit payments affect existing retirees, and they are only a fraction of membership. In short, financial liberalization (or retrenchment) of a retirement system has a lagged rather than an immediate effect.

It may be asked what evidence of significant overall changes is available. For all systems the ratio of beneficiaries to membership rose during the years from 1957 to 1972 from 13.0 percent to 16.1 percent. In 1972, the beneficiary/membership ratio of locally administered systems in eighteen states was about 30.0 percent or more, while this ratio was reached in only one state under state-administered plans. Receipts of all systems grew remarkably, and the growth was attributable, aside from the growth in membership, to growth in the rate of earnings on investments from 2.78 percent in 1957 to 5.05 percent in 1972. This growth was marked by a shift in the composition of assets. In 1957 two-thirds, and in 1972 only 9 percent, of assets were in the form of government securities. The systems had turned sharply to nongovernmental securities, including corporate stocks. Although the shift was not yet complete in 1972, growth in the rate of earnings on investments could not reasonably be expected to continue to rise. The responsibility of providing future payments to beneficiaries will thus fall more heavily on employee and government contributions, mostly on the latter. The governmental contribution has already risen substantially — it was $1,200 million in 1957, $3,055 million in 1967 and $5,750 million in 1972. Governmental contribution has accelerated and seems likely to accelerate further in the years ahead as the systems mature and as benefit provisions are liberalized, especially in response to inflation. No other elastic source for larger receipts will be available.

The caution should be repeated, however, that the significance of these generalizations is diffused because of the diversity of the various funds. Some of the funds recently have strengthened their finances, and the ratio of payments to receipts of funds in the aggregate fell from 40.8 in 1967 to 39.0 in 1972. But the ratio in twenty-three states and the District of Columbia in 1972 exceeded 50.0, and in nine states exceeded 70.0. The sorest spot seems to be the systems of large cities with a declining population. Thirteen of the twenty-nine largest cities in 1972 had ratios of over 50 percent, and nine of them showed a population decline in the decade from 1960 to 1970.

Projecting the financial position of state and local retirement systems through examination of the past record has a serious fault: this record may be a poor indication of what lies ahead. Most of the current disbursements of a retirement system are the result of costs which accrued a generation earlier; they do not reflect costs which will accrue in the future. Prospective disbursements arising out of wage and salary adjustments (which are unlikely to be downward), or benefit improvements in the form of earlier retirement or larger payments, need to be reckoned with. The best device is to apply actuarial methods which estimate the accrual of future costs and translate these costs into present values. This device implies a fully funded system.

Most of the 2,304 state and local retirement systems are partially funded. To ascertain the degree of funding of all of them is impossible within the framework of this study because the individual differences in the systems are many and actuarial reports exist for very few. It is, however, possible to design a present-value model of pension fund financing which can be used to project the potential future fiscal impact of retirement systems on state and local governments. This is the intent of the chapter which follows.

# 4

# PROJECTIONS OF STATE AND LOCAL TRUST FUND FINANCING

*J. Richard Aronson*

This chapter attempts to provide an estimate of the potential fiscal impact of pension plans of state and local governments during the period from 1973 to 1980. Since the task of estimating the costs of each of the 2,304 plans could not be completed within a reasonable period of time, an alternative estimating technique—a simplified present-value model of trust fund financing—has been adopted. On the basis of alternative assumptions on the growth in the dollar value of covered payroll, the level of pension benefits in relation to average salary, on the normal retirement age, and on the level of interest rates, the size of the trust fund needed to meet the obligations of a retirement system can be determined. Target dates can then be established for the accumulation of the needed trust fund assets, and present-value analysis can be used to determine the level of annual payments needed to achieve the goal. The estimates of the needed payments into trust fund accounts can be compared with the actual payments for 1972 to provide some insight into the relationship between trust fund contributions and future obligations.

The first section of this chapter lists the relevant features of a "typical" state and local pension plan. In the second section methods of financing pension plans and intergeneration equity are discussed briefly. The third section presents a model for projecting state and local pension funds and discusses the estimates resulting from the model. The final section provides conclusions.

---

The author wishes to thank Professors Wallace Oates of Princeton University and Daniel Holland of MIT for helpful comments on an earlier version of this chapter, and to thank David Smith for his assistance in programming and running the model developed here.

## The "Typical" State or Local Government Retirement Plan

The retirement system of a state or local government is a complex financial arrangement. A package of benefits must be agreed upon and a financing scheme must be adopted. Eligibility rules for membership must be established. It must be determined whether employees should be accepted into the plan immediately or whether some probationary period should be required. It must be established what kind of benefits should be provided—whether disability, death benefits and survivor benefits should be included or whether the plan should be limited to providing pensions to retirees. It must be agreed whether the level of pension benefits should be set as a fraction of the employee's average salary or whether benefits should be determined by the future value of the periodic contributions made by the employee and his government employer. Vesting provisions must be set up.[1] Retirement age must be established, and whether early retirement should be permitted must be decided.

As noted in Chapter 3, there is a wide variety of methods for financing a retirement system. At one extreme, there is pay-as-you-go finance and, at the other extreme, is the actuarial method referred to as the fully funded approach. No matter what financing scheme is adopted, what must be decided in each case is the relative contribution of employees and government.

As was also pointed out in the previous chapter, retirement systems contain so many features that it is not surprising to find wide variations in the plans adopted by state and local governments. Yet it is possible to describe some of the features of what might be considered a "typical" plan. Robert Tilove, in a recent study of state-local retirement systems, surveyed a large number of plans and suggested that the following features may be considered typical.[2]

*Benefit formula.* An employee's annual pension is determined by multiplying the number of years he has worked by 1.67 percent of his final average salary. This means that an individual who has worked for thirty years retires with a pension equal to 50 percent of his final average salary. Final average salary is an average of the employee's five highest-paid years in his last ten years of service.

---

[1] Vesting refers to the attainment by a participant of a benefit right, attributable to employer contributions, that is not contingent upon a participant's continuation in specified employment. See J. J. Melone and E. T. Allen, *Pension Planning* (Homewood, Ill.: Richard D. Irwin, 1966), p. 53, and *Bulletin of the Commission on Insurance Terminology of the American Risk and Insurance Association*, vol. 1, no. 4.

[2] Robert Tilove, "Study of Public Employee Retirement Systems," The Twentieth Century Fund, 1974, processed, Chapter 2.

*Cost-of-living adjustment.* Pension benefits are guaranteed to increase with the consumer price index up to a maximum of 3 percent per year.

*Retirement age.* The normal retirement age is sixty if the employee has at least ten years of service and with ten years of service the employee may retire at age fifty-five on a reduced early retirement pension. There is compulsory retirement at age seventy.

*Vesting.* If an employee leaves after ten years of service and does not withdraw his contributions, he is entitled to normal pension benefits at age sixty or early retirement benefits at age fifty-five. This means that the government's contributions become vested in the employee after ten years of service.

*Disability benefit.* A disability pension is provided for those who have at least ten years of service. The benefit is guaranteed to be not less than 25 percent of final average salary unless that amount exceeds what the employee would receive under normal retirement at age sixty. The service requirement is waived if the disability was the result of a job-connected accident.

*Death benefits.* The typical plan includes a variety of death benefits. If an employee dies after at least one year of employment, his beneficiary is entitled to a half year's salary. If he has been employed for ten years, the benefit is usually a full year's salary. If the employee dies at a time he is eligible to retire, his widow is entitled to an annuity equal to what she would have received if he had retired just before his death.

Some 160 of the largest systems, representing about 80 percent of the total membership in retirement plans, use the actuarially determined rates with the objective of becoming fully funded.[3]

## Methods of Funding and Intergeneration Equity

As noted, the alternative schemes for financing a pension system range between pay-as-you-go finance and the fully funded approach. From a narrow point of view, the cost of a pension plan to the community as a whole is the same no matter what financing scheme is adopted. The simple example shown in Table 4–1 demonstrates the point. A governmental unit enters into a pension arrangement with some of

[3] See *State and Local Employee Pension Systems* (New York: Tax Foundation, Inc., 1969), pp. 28-29

## Table 4–1

PRESENT VALUE OF PENSION BENEFITS

(dollars)

| | | Pay-As-You-Go | | Fully Funded | | | | |
|---|---|---|---|---|---|---|---|---|
| | **Pension Benefits** (1) | Gov't payments (2a) | Present value of payments $i=.05$ (2b) | Lump sum (3a) | Annual contributions (3b) | Value of trust fund before pension payment (4a) | Pension payment (4b) | Value of trust fund after pension payment (4c) |
| $t_1$ | 0 | 0 | 0 | 160.70 | 45.32 | | | |
| $t_2$ | 0 | 0 | 0 | | 45.32 | | | |
| $t_3$ | 0 | 0 | 0 | | 45.32 | | | |
| $t_4$ | 100 | 100 | 82.30 | | 45.32 | 195.33 | 100.00 | 95.33 |
| $t_5$ | 100 | 100 | 78.40 | | | 100.00 | 100.00 | 0 |
| $t_6$ | 0 | 0 | 0 | | | | | |
| . | . | . | . | | | | | |
| . | . | . | . | | | | | |
| . | . | . | . | | | | | |
| . | . | . | . | | | | | |
| . | . | . | . | | | | | |
| $t_n$ | 0 | 0 | 0 | | | | | |
| Present value with $i=.05$ | | | 160.70 | 160.70 | 160.70 | | | |

its employees and according to best estimates it is expected that the payments to pensioners will be zero in the first three periods, $100 in periods four and five and zero thereafter. Assume the government will pay the full costs of the plan. If the plan is financed on a pay-as-you-go basis (column 2a), the government will have to make payments of $100 in years four and five. With a 5 percent rate of discount, the present value (column 2b) or cost of this plan is $160.70.

The government might, however, consider funding the pension plan with a single lump-sum contribution at the time the plan is initiated (column 3a). The amount needed to cover all of the obligations of the plan is, of course, $160.70, which is the same as the cost of the plan under pay-as-you-go. Assuming a 5 percent rate of interest, $160.70 will grow to $195.33 by the end of the fourth period (column 4a). At the end of period four, $100 must be paid to pensioners, leaving $95.33 in the trust fund. At a 5 percent rate of interest $95.33 grows to $100 by the end of period five, providing exactly the amount needed for pensioners. The amount needed by the end of period four ($195.33) to finance the benefits could be accumulated by a system of equal annual contributions as well as by a single lump-sum payment. Column (3b) shows equal annual contributions of $45.32 over four periods. Assuming a 5 percent rate of interest, these contributions grow to $195.33 by the end of period four. The cost to the government of this plan is the same as the cost of the other two plans. The present value of four payments of $45.32 at a 5 percent rate of discount is $160.70.

However, the fact that the present value of the future obligations of a pension plan is not affected by the method of finance does not mean that the schemes are equally satisfactory. A pay-as-you-go system has some undesirable features. For example, for the pension plans of private firms, pure pay-as-you-go financing offers no security to the claims of pensioners. If the fortunes of the firm were to take a bad turn there would be pressure on the firm to renege on its promise and reduce the level of pension benefits. If the firm were to go bankrupt the claims of pensioners would be worthless. Under the trust fund (fully funded) approach the assets of the retirement system would be segregated from the other assets of the firm and as a result the claims of the pensioners would be protected.[4]

The chance of a state or city ceasing operations is slight. Moreover, the rights of public employees to their pensions are protected

[4] Of course, it is impossible to provide perfect protection for the claims of pensioners. Trust fund assets can be mismanaged and private insurance companies can fail.

by law. Thus, the reasons for using the trust fund (fully funded) approach in public employee retirement systems must be something other than the protection of the claims of retired and active workers. The trust fund (fully funded) approach is preferable to a pay-as-you-go approach because some degree of intergeneration equity between present and future taxpayers is assured and because the governmental unit is protected from potential fiscal strain.

The problem of intergeneration equity is seen most clearly if one focuses attention on the government's financial obligations to the plan. Under pay-as-you-go, the pension benefits due in each year are financed by general taxation in that year. Tax rates to finance pension benefits need not rise over time as long as the tax base (income and wealth of the community) rises at a rate higher than the rate at which pension benefits rise. Continuous growth in the wealth of states and cities, however, is not to be expected. Some states and cities will experience a decrease in their population and their tax base. Under these conditions it is likely that the number of public employees and membership in retirement plans will eventually fall. Nevertheless, the level of pension benefits will not decrease for a considerable period of time. If one assumes that any existing employee contribution rate is held constant and that there is no trust fund, he must conclude that the burden of the pension plan would be felt in the form of higher tax rates. Pay-as-you-go will present a problem of intergeneration equity, since, to support the plan, future residents of the community will face higher tax rates than current residents. Moreover, the necessary increase in tax rates, at a time when the tax base is shrinking, will aggravate the fiscal problems of the community and for smaller governmental units may even lead to further reductions in the tax base.[5]

The trust fund (fully funded) approach avoids these problems. Since the employee and government (taxpayers) contribute to the fund when pension liabilities accrue rather than when the actual payments must be made, intergeneration equity is preserved.[6] Moreover, higher future tax rates to finance benefits are not inevitable when the tax

[5] For an analysis of how changes in tax rates can induce changes in the tax base of a community, see J. R. Aronson and E. Schwartz, "Financing Public Goods and the Distribution of Population in a System of Local Governments," *National Tax Journal*, June 1973, pp. 137-60.

[6] At the time when the plan is initiated or when benefit provisions are liberalized existing employees are given past service credits even though no contributions have been made in their behalf. This financial obligation is usually referred to as a supplemental unfunded balance and generally amortized over a rather lengthy period. This procedure creates difficulties in achieving intergeneration equity because beneficiaries are given pension credits the costs of which must be spread over future generations.

base of the governmental unit declines. The trust fund and its interest earnings along with a constant government contribution rate based on covered payroll provide the funds to meet benefit payments. As long as the community tax base does not decrease at a faster rate than covered payroll, tax rates need not rise.

## A Model for Projecting State-Local Pension Funds

The purpose of this section is to develop a model of pension fund financing that can be used to project the future fiscal impact of retirement systems on state and local governments. In general, for a pension plan to be fully funded the value of the trust fund (*TF*) should be equal to the discounted stream of future pension benefits less the discounted stream of future contributions. That is,

$$TF = \sum_{n=1}^{\infty} \frac{B_n - C_n}{(1+i)^n} \tag{4.1}$$

where

- $B_n$ is the total amount of pension benefit payments in year $n$,
- $C_n$ is the total contributions (of employees and the government) in year $n$,
- $i$ is the interest rate (that is, the assumed rate of return on trust fund assets).

Since the size of the trust fund needed to achieve a fully funded position depends on the future stream of benefits and contributions, it is necessary to make a number of assumptions about the future. In estimating $B_n$ and $C_n$ mortality rates must be assumed, and if a probationary period is required before government contributions are vested in the employee, withdrawal rates should be taken into account. The rate of return in equation (4.1) is the assumed rate of earnings on trust fund assets.[7]

As membership in the plan grows or as benefit provisions are liberalized the size of the trust fund must increase if the plan is to remain fully funded. Thus, to estimate the future costs of retirement systems requires assumptions of growth in membership and improvements in benefit provisions. There are conditions under which the trust fund would reach a maximum value. Consider, for example, a retirement system in which the number of employed members is

---

[7] Since it is to be expected that the actual experience of any system will deviate from the assumed conditions it is necessary periodically to recalculate the value of the needed trust fund.

constant (that is, each year the newly hired employees equal the number retiring), and the number retiring is equal to the number dying. Assume also that the total dollar payroll of covered employees is constant and that pensions are set as a percent of the employee's average salary. A retirement system with these characteristics would be called "mature" and the plan would be considered fully funded if the size of the trust fund were:

$$MTF = \sum_{n=1}^{d} \frac{B_n}{(1+i)^n} - \sum_{n=1}^{R} \frac{C_n}{(1+i)^n}. \qquad (4.2)$$

The mature trust fund ($MTF$) is the hypothetical maximum trust fund that exists under a given set of actuarial assumptions; it contains sufficient funds to phase out the program and cover all of the plan's obligations, even if membership in the system declines or no new members are accepted at all. That is to say, the funds derived from drawing down trust fund assets—along with the interest on the declining assets and with the annual contributions from the declining covered payroll—will be sufficient to cover the plan's liabilities. Equation (4.2) shows that a mature retirement system is fully funded when the value of the mature trust fund ($MTF$) is equal to the present value of the pension payments to all members of the system until the last member has died ($n=d$) less the present value of annual contributions until the last employed member retires ($n=R$).[8]

It is convenient to state the annual contributions as a percent of the covered payroll. If the annual contributions to a mature retirement system are to be a constant percent ($a$) of covered payroll ($PR_n$) then

$$C_n = aPR_n \qquad (4.3)$$

and substituting (4.3) into (4.2) yields

$$MTF = \sum_{n=1}^{d} \frac{B_n}{(1+i)^n} - \sum_{n=1}^{R} \frac{aPR_n}{(1+i)^n}. \qquad (4.4)$$

During the period of time over which the retirement system remains mature the level of the trust fund should be constant. There is no need for the fund to increase or decrease during this period: membership, payroll, annual benefits and annual contributions are all assumed constant.[9]

---

[8] The contributions may be divided among employees and the government.

[9] It should be noted that the mature retirement system is defined to be constant in both the level of membership and the amount of covered payroll. It is possible, of course, to have a system in which the membership is constant but the payroll increases. Under these conditions the $MTF$ would also have to increase.

For the mature trust fund to remain constant,

$$iMTF + a\,\mathbf{P} = B_c\,. \tag{4.5}$$

Equation (4.5) shows that interest on the mature trust fund with the annual contributions based on the maximum and constant covered payroll (**P**) is just sufficient to meet the constant stream of pension payments ($B_c$) that must be met as long as the system remains in a mature state.

Equation (4.5) may be rewritten to solve for the contribution rate ($a$):

$$a = \frac{B_c}{\mathbf{P}} - \frac{iMTF}{\mathbf{P}}. \tag{4.6}$$

Since both $B_c$ and **P** are constants, $B_c/\mathbf{P} = b$ and equation (4.6) may be simplified to

$$a = b - \frac{iMTF}{\mathbf{P}}. \tag{4.6a}$$

Equation (4.6a) may be substituted into equation (4.4) to produce

$$MTF = \sum_{n=1}^{d} \frac{B_n}{(1+i)^n} - \sum_{n=1}^{R} \frac{(b - \frac{iMTF}{\mathbf{P}})\ PR_n}{(1+i)^n}, \tag{4.7}$$

and if (4.7) is rearranged to solve for the $MTF$ we have

$$MTF = \frac{\sum_{n=1}^{d} \frac{B_n}{(1+i)^n} - \sum_{n=1}^{R} \frac{bPR_n}{(1+i)^n}}{1 - \frac{i}{\mathbf{P}} \sum_{n=1}^{R} \frac{PR_n}{(1+i)^n}}. \tag{4.8}$$

The value of the $MTF$ is the amount that must eventually be accumulated in the trust fund of a mature retirement system. In what follows an estimate is made of the annual payments to trust fund accounts needed to accumulate these assets by the year 2000.[10] The level of the annual payments depends on the value of the current unfunded balance ($UB$) which is defined by equation (4.9) where $CA$ represents the assets already accumulated in the trust fund and $y$ is the amortization period over which the unfunded balance is to be eliminated:

$$UB = MTF - CA(1+i)^y. \tag{4.9}$$

[10] The following section presents a series of $MTF$ estimates (based on alternative actuarial assumptions). The effects of changes in the length of the amortization period are also analyzed.

The size of the annual payment is identical with the annuity whose future value is equal to the unfunded balance. For example, if the current time is the end of 1972 and the goal is to accumulate the mature trust fund assets by the beginning of the year 2000, the unfunded balance is calculated by subtracting the value of the assets held in the trust fund as of the end of 1972 and the interest earnings on these assets for twenty-seven years from the value of the mature trust fund.[11] For the determination of the level of annual payments ($An$) to the trust fund, the unfunded balance is amortized over twenty-seven years:

$$An = \frac{UB}{\frac{(1+i)^y - 1}{i}} \cdot \tag{4.10}$$

It should be noted that $An$ represents only the incremental payments to the trust fund and that until the assets required for the mature trust fund are accumulated the overall contribution rate must be set at such a level sufficient to pay annual pension benefits and provide the amount $An$. When the mature trust fund has been achieved, $An$ will equal zero and the annual contributions plus the interest earnings on the $MTF$ will be sufficient to finance annual benefits.

## Simulated Projection of the Model

Equation (4.8) has been used to project mature trust fund levels for state and local retirement systems. It is assumed that each state has one plan covering all state and local employees. The plan includes only pension benefits and no employee probationary period is required for acceptance in the plan. A simulation approach is used. For each state, the $MTF$ level is calculated under alternative assumptions on the interest rate, the maximum level of the covered payroll, and the retirement age. The procedure provides a range of estimates for each state. So many simplifying assumptions are necessary, however, that the results must be used with extreme caution.

Calculating the $MTF$ for each state requires that estimates be made for $\mathbf{P}$, $B_n$, $d$, $b$, $PR_n$, $R$ and $i$. These estimates have been made in the following fashion.

[11] It is assumed that interest earnings on trust fund assets stay in the trust fund (that is, they are not used to finance payments to beneficiaries) until the system is fully funded.

The maximum covered payroll (**P**) is estimated by assuming that the covered payroll increases at a constant rate for a number of years and then levels off. Alternative assumptions are made as to when the system matures. The starting point is established from actual payroll data for 1971, and for the calculations in this chapter it is assumed that the payroll increases at an annual rate of 11.2 percent for ten years and then remains at this constant maximum level.[12] This provides a measure of **P** needed to calculate the *MTF*. Values are calculated for **P** and the resulting *MTF* under the alternative assumptions that the annual rate of increase in payroll continues for eleven, twelve, thirteen, fourteen, or fifteen years. These assumptions should not be interpreted as implying that the rate of increase in salaries after fifteen years of growth will necessarily be zero: the assumptions merely provide a planning horizon for the funding policy of the retirement system.[13]

Since the size of a mature trust fund is being estimated, $B_n$ represents the stream of future pension payments that will occur once the plan stops accepting new members.[14] If one assumes that employed members range in age from twenty-five to sixty-five, that there is an equal number of people in each age category, and that every employee retires at age sixty-five, he can expect that pension payments will remain constant at the level $B_c$ for about forty years. After forty years, all covered employees will have retired or died and diminishing annual pension payments will be made until the last retired worker dies. This period is assumed to be ten years and thus $d$ is assumed

[12] The assumed annual rate of increase in covered payroll of 11.2 percent is composed of an assumed rate of increase in state and local employment of 4.2 percent per year and a 7 percent rate of increase in average wages and salaries per year (4 percent for inflation and 3 percent for productivity growth). In Chapter 5, the simulations allow for different rates of growth of state and local government employment and different rates of inflation.

[13] Salary increases to compensate for inflation may occur well beyond the fifteen-year period of assumed payroll growth. To determine the net effect of such inflationary increases on the *MTF* it would be necessary to estimate the period over which such inflation is expected (perhaps perpetual inflation should be assumed) and determine the effect of inflation on the rate of earnings on trust fund assets.

[14] It should be remembered that in the terminology of this study a mature trust fund is the hypothetical maximum trust fund that exists under a given set of actuarial assumptions. When the system begins to contract (membership is declining), the interest earnings on the trust fund assets with the current contributions based on a constant percent of a falling covered payroll will not be sufficient to cover the annual pension payments. Under these conditions the trust fund assets must be drawn down. The *MTF*, equation (4.8), provides the amount which when added to interest earnings and current contributions provides exactly the amount needed to pay off all the obligations of the plan.

to be the fiftieth year. Projections are also made on the assumption that the retirement age is sixty rather than sixty-five. Under these conditions it is reasonable to expect that the level of pension payments would remain constant for about thirty-five years and diminish to zero over the next fifteen years. In this case also, $d$ represents the fiftieth year.[15]

The constant $b = \frac{B_c}{\mathbf{P}}$ is the maximum annual pension payment as a percent of the maximum payroll: it is set at 20 percent when it is assumed employees retire at age sixty-five and at 30 percent when the retirement age is sixty. The value of $b$ has been obtained by an estimate of the ratio of retired workers to employed workers in the future and the assumption that an employee's pension will be equal to his average salary. According to Census Bureau projections the ratio of the number of people sixty-five years and older to the number of people age twenty-five to sixty-four will remain reasonably level at 22 percent until the end of the century; and the ratio of the number of people sixty and over to the number of people twenty-five to sixty will be about 34 percent.[16] These ratios can be used to approximate the ratio ($b$) if (1) the age profile of state and local employees is similar to the age profile of the entire nation, (2) the pensions paid to workers are set equal to their average salary, and (3) there is no significant variation in life expectancy of workers in different occupations and earnings categories within the state. Because these assumptions are tenuous the value of $b$ is set at 20 percent or 30 percent rather than at 22 percent or 34 percent.

The annual covered payroll ($PR_n$) begins to diminish as soon as the plan stops accepting new members. It has been assumed that the youngest employees are twenty-five years old. Thus, if retirement is at age sixty-five, the covered payroll will decrease to zero over forty years and if retirement is at age sixty, the covered payroll will decrease to zero over thirty-five years. In the calculation of the *MTF* in equation (4.8), $R$ is the fortieth year when the retirement age is sixty-five and $R$ is the thirty-fifth year when the retirement age is sixty. For ease

[15] The assumptions, that benefit payments remain constant for either thirty-five or forty years and then diminish in equal increments to zero over the next fifteen or ten years, are made for the sake of convenience of calculation. However, since benefits have been time-discounted over a period of fifty years, the differences between the actual time path of benefit payments and the time path assumed should not significantly affect the value of the *MTF*.

[16] See U.S. Department of Commerce, *Statistical Abstract of the United States* (Washington, D. C., 1970), pp. 8-9, and *Facts and Figures on Government Finance: 17th Biennial Edition* (New York: Tax Foundation, Inc., 1973), p. 40.

of calculation it is assumed that the covered payroll diminishes in equal increments over the appropriate time period. The estimates of the *MTF* are based on assumed interest rates of 4 percent, 5 percent and 6 percent.

For each state there are thirty-six different estimates of the mature trust fund. The summary tabulation in Table 4–2 shows how these are arranged. System A refers to pension plans that assume retirement at age sixty-five; system B refers to those plans that assume retirement at age sixty. For each assumed interest rate (6 percent, 5 percent, 4 percent), there are six estimated values of the mature trust fund based on alternative assumptions as to how long the covered payroll can be expected to increase at a constant annual rate of 11.2 percent—ten years, eleven years, twelve years, thirteen years, fourteen years or fifteen years.

Table 4–3 shows the thirty-six estimated mature trust fund values for all state and local governments combined. The lowest value, $560.8 billion, occurs under the assumptions that retirement takes place at age sixty-five, that covered payroll increases at a constant annual rate of 11.2 percent for only ten years from its 1971 level,[17] and that the interest earned on trust fund assets is 6 percent. The highest value, $1,716.3 billion, is based on retirement at age sixty, an increase in covered payroll for fifteen years from its 1971 level, and an interest rate of 4 percent. In general, for any given interest rate, the value of the mature trust fund is higher the longer the assumed period of payroll growth; and for any given assumed period of payroll growth, the value of the mature trust fund is higher the lower the interest rate.

**Table 4–2**

CLASSIFICATION OF PENSION PLAN SIMULATION ASSUMPTIONS

| System | Interest Rate | Number of Years Payroll Assumed to Increase at a Constant Annual Rate of 11.2% |
|---|---|---|
| System A: Retirement at age sixty-five | 6%<br>5%<br>4% | 10, 11, 12, 13, 14, 15 |
| System B: Retirement at age sixty | 6%<br>5%<br>4% | 10, 11, 12, 13, 14, 15 |

[17] The 1971 payroll estimates by state are found in the appendix to this chapter.

## Table 4–3

ESTIMATED VALUES OF MATURE TRUST FUND AND UNFUNDED BALANCE: ALL STATE AND LOCAL GOVERNMENTS COMBINED

($ billions)

| System | Interest Rate | Number of Years of Growth in Covered Payroll[a] 10 | 11 | 12 | 13 | 14 | 15 |
|---|---|---|---|---|---|---|---|
| | | Value of mature trust fund | | | | | |
| A | 6 | 560.8 | 623.7 | 693.5 | 771.2 | 857.6 | 953.6 |
| | 5 | 618.6 | 687.9 | 764.9 | 850.6 | 945.9 | 1,051.8 |
| | 4 | 684.2 | 760.8 | 846.0 | 940.8 | 1,046.2 | 1,163.3 |
| B | 6 | 827.6 | 920.3 | 1,023.4 | 1,138.0 | 1,265.5 | 1,407.2 |
| | 5 | 912.4 | 1,014.6 | 1,128.2 | 1,254.6 | 1,395.1 | 1,551.3 |
| | 4 | 1,009.4 | 1,122.5 | 1,248.2 | 1,388.0 | 1,543.5 | 1,716.3 |
| | | Unfunded balance[b] | | | | | |
| A | 6 | 229.3 | 292.1 | 361.9 | 439.6 | 526.0 | 622.0 |
| | 5 | 361.9 | 431.2 | 508.2 | 593.9 | 689.2 | 795.1 |
| | 4 | 485.9 | 562.6 | 647.8 | 742.5 | 847.9 | 965.1 |
| B | 6 | 496.0 | 588.7 | 691.8 | 806.4 | 933.9 | 1,075.6 |
| | 5 | 655.7 | 757.9 | 871.5 | 997.8 | 1,138.4 | 1,294.6 |
| | 4 | 811.2 | 924.2 | 1,050.0 | 1,189.8 | 1,345.2 | 1,518.1 |

[a] Covered payroll assumed to increase at an annual rate of 11.2 percent.

[b] The unfunded balance is equal to the mature trust fund less the future value (in the year 2000) of actual cash and security holdings in trust fund accounts as of 1971.

**Source:** Author's estimates.

The *MTF* is an estimate of the cash and security holdings that must eventually be accumulated in the retirement trust fund. In order to measure the future fiscal impact of retirement systems, the value of the mature trust fund should be compared with the amount of cash and securities currently held in the system. Total cash and security holdings for all state and local government retirement systems at the end of 1972 were $68.8 billion.[18] It is, of course, both unreasonable and unnecessary to expect that the difference between the value of the mature trust fund and current amount of cash and securities held by public retirement systems be contributed immediately in a single

[18] The 1972 year-end value of trust fund assets by state is found in Table A-1 of this chapter.

lump-sum payment. However, a target date should be established for the achievement of the necessary level of trust fund assets.

In addition to presenting the *MTF* estimates, Table 4–3 also shows thirty-six estimates of the unfunded balance. To calculate the unfunded balance it is assumed that the target date for the accumulation of the assets needed in the mature trust fund is the year 2000. The unfunded balance is measured by subtracting the value of the current cash and security holdings and the interest earnings on these assets for twenty-seven years, that is, \$68.8 billion $\times$ $(1 + i)^{27}$, from the value of the mature trust fund. The assumption here is that during the period from the end of 1972 to the beginning of the year 2000 the interest earnings on trust fund assets will be used to build up the fund rather than to pay annual benefits.

The annual payments needed to amortize the unfunded balances are shown in Table 4–4. Given the year 2000 as the target date, the unfunded balance would be amortized over twenty-seven years.

**Table 4–4**

ESTIMATED NECESSARY NET ANNUAL PAYMENTS TO PUBLIC RETIREMENT SYSTEM TRUST FUNDS: ALL STATE AND LOCAL GOVERNMENTS COMBINED[a]

(\$ millions)

| System | Interest Rate | Number of Years of Growth in Covered Payroll | | | | | |
|---|---|---|---|---|---|---|---|
| | | 10 | 11 | 12 | 13 | 14 | 15 |
| | 6 | 3,598.7 | 4,584.7 | 5,681.1 | 6,900.4 | 8,256.2 | 9,763.8 |
| A | 5 | 6,619.7 | 7,887.1 | 9,296.4 | 10,863.5 | 12,606.1 | 14.543.9 |
| | 4 | 10,320.5 | 11,948.0 | 13,757.8 | 15,770.3 | 18,008.2 | 20,496.7 |
| | 6 | 3,598.7 | 3,999.9 | 4,446.3 | 4,942.5 | 5,494.4 | 6,108.2 |
| A′ | 5 | 6,619.7 | 7,200.2 | 7,848.7 | 8,572.6 | 9,380.5 | 10,281.6 |
| | 4 | 10,320.5 | 11,147.6 | 12,074.2 | 13,111.5 | 14,271.7 | 15,568.4 |
| | 6 | 7,786.3 | 9,241.3 | 10,859.3 | 12,658.5 | 14,659.2 | 16,884.0 |
| B | 5 | 11,993.3 | 13,862.5 | 15,941.1 | 18,252.4 | 20,822.4 | 23,680.6 |
| | 4 | 17,228.2 | 19,629.4 | 22,299.5 | 25,268.6 | 28,570.3 | 32,241.8 |
| | 6 | 7,786.3 | 8,339.6 | 8,959.9 | 9,654.6 | 10,432.0 | 11,301.2 |
| B′ | 5 | 11,993.3 | 12,808.7 | 13,725.0 | 14,753.4 | 15,906.4 | 17,197.5 |
| | 4 | 17,228.2 | 18,405.9 | 19,731.5 | 21,221.1 | 22,893.0 | 24,767.0 |

[a] The estimates for system A and B are derived by amortizing the unfunded balances of Table 4–3 over twenty-seven years.

**Source:** Author's estimates.

There is a wide range of values in Table 4–4. The low estimate calls for twenty-seven annual payments of $3,598.7 million in order to cover plans for retirement at age sixty-five, a 6 percent interest rate and a ten-year period of growth in covered payroll. The high estimate is twenty-seven annual payments of $32,241.8 million in order to finance plans with retirement at age sixty, an interest rate of 4 percent and a fifteen-year period of payroll growth.

The annual payments reported in Table 4–4 are the amounts that should be added annually to the retirement systems' trust funds for all state and local governments combined. These estimated amounts can be compared with the actual contributions to state and local systems. In 1972, for all state and local governments combined, the contribution to trust funds was $4,230.1 million.[19] Thirty-five of the thirty-six estimates of systems A and B exceed this amount. This comparison should not be taken to imply irresponsible fiscal behavior on the part of state and local governments. The model has been built on a hypothetical pension plan rather than on actual plans; each state is assumed to have only one plan covering all state and local employees; an employee's pension benefit is set equal to his average salary; and a twenty-seven year amortization period is assumed.

Comparison of the various estimated annual contributions with the actual level of contributions may, however, provide some insight into the potential fiscal pressure that retirement systems will exert on state and local governments. As noted earlier, two typical features of actual pension plans (according to Tilove) are retirement at age sixty and pension payments equal to 50 percent of final average salary. Thus, the system-B estimates of Table 4–4 would seem to be the more appropriate.[20] Under system B the necessary annual addition to the trust fund ranges from a low of $7,786.3 million to a high of $32,241.8 million. It would therefore appear that the goal of retirement of employees at age sixty with a pension approximately equal to average pay will require state and local governments for the next twenty-seven

[19] U.S. Bureau of the Census, *Government Finances in the U.S., Finances of Employee-Retirement Systems of State and Local Governments* (Washington, D.C.: Government Printing Office, 1972). In 1972, retirement system revenues less expenditures were $7,700.7 million and of this amount $3,470.6 million were earnings on trust fund assets. The annual payment to be compared with the estimates in Table 4–4 was, therefore, $4,230.1 million.

[20] The hypothetical plan sets pension benefits equal to 100 percent of average salary which is higher than 50 percent of final average salary. However, during recent years there has been a trend toward making benefit provisions of pension plans more generous. Moreover, although most actual plans require a probationary period before vesting occurs, they also include other benefits (death, disability, early retirement benefits) which have not been taken into account here.

years to add somewhere between $3,556.2 million and $28,011.7 million per year over and above what they are already adding to their trust fund accounts.

The fiscal implications of trust fund financing can be looked at from another point of view. To this point a twenty-seven-year amortization period has been used. However, the longer the amortization period the lower will be the annual contributions needed to eliminate an unfunded balance. Since the 1972 contribution to state and local retirement systems was $4,320.1 million, it is reasonable to ask how many years of contributions at this level would be needed to eliminate the unfunded balance. Table 4–5 shows the implicit amortization

**Table 4–5**

IMPLICIT AMORTIZATION PERIODS OF UNFUNDED BALANCES IF ANNUAL PAYMENT TO TRUST FUND IS $4,230.1 MILLION[a]

| | | Number of Years of Growth in Covered Payroll | | | | | |
|---|---|---|---|---|---|---|---|
| **System** | **Interest Rate** | 10 | 11 | 12 | 13 | 14 | 15 |
| A | 6 | 25.9 | 27.6 | 29.2 | 30.9 | 32.5 | 34.2 |
| | 5 | 31.2 | 33.1 | 35.1 | 37.1 | 39.0 | 41.0 |
| | 4 | 38.5 | 40.9 | 43.3 | 45.7 | 48.1 | 50.6 |
| B | 6 | 32.0 | 33.7 | 35.4 | 37.1 | 38.8 | 40.5 |
| | 5 | 38.4 | 40.4 | 42.4 | 44.4 | 46.5 | 48.5 |
| | 4 | 47.3 | 49.8 | 52.2 | 54.8 | 57.3 | 59.8 |

[a] The estimates in this table are based on the assumptions that the current level of trust fund assets is $68,760.3 million and that the annual contribution is $4,320.1 million. The implicit amortization period can be determined by solving equation (1) for *n*.

$$68{,}760.3(1+i)^n + \frac{4{,}320.1\,[(1+i)^n - 1]}{i} = A \qquad (1)$$

where *A* is the value of the mature trust fund shown in Table 4–3.

Rearranging the terms in (1) and setting $\left[\dfrac{A + \dfrac{4{,}320.1}{i}}{68{,}760.3 + \dfrac{4{,}320.1}{i}}\right] = Z$

provides the solution for *n*.

$$n = \frac{\ln Z}{\ln(1+i)} \qquad (2)$$

The solution for *n* gives the number of years it will take for the sum of the current assets growing at a given interest rate and the annual contributions plus interest on these contributions to reach the level of the mature trust fund.

periods for the mature trust fund estimates of systems A and B under the assumptions that the current value of trust fund assets is $68.8 billion and that the annual contributions to the trust fund will remain $4,320.1 million. The estimates run from 25.9 years to 59.8 years. Thus, it appears that under plausible assumptions, it will be necessary to maintain large surpluses in the trust fund accounts far into the future.

For systems A and B the year 2000 is the target date for eliminating the unfunded balance. As time passes, however, and as the financial position of retirement systems is reevaluated, it may not be unreasonable to push the target date further into the future and thereby lengthen the amortization period.

For systems A′ (retirement at age sixty-five) and B′ (retirement at age sixty), as each year passes an additional year of payroll growth is anticipated and the target date for eliminating the unfunded balance is pushed one year further into the future. For example, assume it is 1973 and that ten years of payroll growth and a 6 percent rate of interest are anticipated. The value of the unfunded balance for all state and local governments under system B would be $496.0 billion (Table 4–3) and annual payments of $7,786.3 million would be required to amortize the unfunded balance over twenty-seven years (Table 4–4, system B or B′). At the beginning of the next year, 1974, the retirement system is reevaluated and an additional year of payroll growth is now anticipated, thus raising the level of the *MTF*. If $7,786.3 million were actually contributed to the fund in 1973 the unfunded balance as of 1974 would be $531.3 million. If this amount is amortized over twenty-seven years (the target date is now the year 2001 rather than 2000), the annual payment under system B′ would be $8,339.6 million compared to $9,241.3 million under system B. The lower payment would result from the extension of the amortization period for an extra year each year. In general, the annual contributions called for under system B′ would be lower than those called for under system B. Moreover, the financing procedure described by system B′ probably reflects the actual financing practices of state and local governments more accurately than does the procedure described by system B.

Table 4–6 gives estimates of the required mature trust fund (*MTF*) for systems A and B on a state-by-state basis. Only the estimates for ten years and fifteen years of payroll growth have been included. Table 4–7 shows the annual payments needed to amortize the unfunded balance under systems A, A′, B and B′. The lowest estimated annual payments are found in column (1) and arise from

## Table 4–6

MATURE TRUST FUND ESTIMATES BY STATE

($ billions)

SYSTEM A

**Number of Years of Growth in Covered Payroll, Various Interest Rates**

| | 6% | | 5% | | 4% | |
|---|---|---|---|---|---|---|
| | 10 | 15 | 10 | 15 | 10 | 15 |
| Alabama | 6.79 | 11.55 | 7.49 | 12.74 | 8.29 | 14.09 |
| Alaska | 1.81 | 3.08 | 2.00 | 3.40 | 2.21 | 3.76 |
| Arizona | 5.54 | 9.42 | 6.11 | 10.39 | 6.76 | 11.50 |
| Arkansas | 3.14 | 5.34 | 3.47 | 5.89 | 3.83 | 6.52 |
| California | 72.76 | 123.71 | 80.25 | 136.45 | 88.76 | 150.92 |
| Colorado | 6.59 | 11.21 | 7.27 | 12.37 | 8.04 | 13.68 |
| Connecticut | 8.45 | 14.37 | 9.32 | 15.85 | 10.31 | 17.53 |
| Delaware | 1.63 | 2.77 | 1.80 | 3.06 | 1.99 | 3.38 |
| Florida | 17.79 | 30.25 | 19.63 | 33.37 | 21.71 | 36.91 |
| Georgia | 10.18 | 17.31 | 11.23 | 19.09 | 12.42 | 21.12 |
| Hawaii | 2.86 | 4.87 | 3.16 | 5.37 | 3.49 | 5.94 |
| Idaho | 1.64 | 2.78 | 1.81 | 3.07 | 2.00 | 3.40 |
| Illinois | 31.63 | 53.78 | 34.89 | 59.32 | 38.59 | 65.61 |
| Indiana | 11.73 | 19.94 | 12.94 | 22.00 | 14.31 | 24.33 |
| Iowa | 7.04 | 11.97 | 7.76 | 13.20 | 8.59 | 14.60 |
| Kansas | 5.57 | 9.47 | 6.14 | 10.44 | 6.79 | 11.55 |
| Kentucky | 6.22 | 10.57 | 6.86 | 11.66 | 7.58 | 12.89 |
| Louisiana | 8.56 | 14.56 | 9.45 | 16.06 | 10.45 | 17.77 |
| Maine | 2.10 | 3.58 | 2.32 | 3.95 | 2.57 | 4.30 |
| Maryland | 11.65 | 19.82 | 12.86 | 21.86 | 14.22 | 24.18 |
| Massachusetts | 16.27 | 27.66 | 17.94 | 30.51 | 19.85 | 33.75 |
| Michigan | 27.72 | 47.13 | 30.58 | 51.99 | 33.82 | 57.50 |
| Minnesota | 11.30 | 19.21 | 12.46 | 21.19 | 13.78 | 23.44 |
| Mississippi | 4.01 | 6.81 | 4.42 | 7.51 | 4.89 | 8.31 |
| Missouri | 10.53 | 17.91 | 11.62 | 19.76 | 12.85 | 21.85 |
| Montana | 1.90 | 3.23 | 2.10 | 3.56 | 2.32 | 3.94 |
| Nebraska | 3.87 | 6.57 | 4.26 | 7.25 | 4.72 | 8.02 |
| Nevada | 1.82 | 3.09 | 2.01 | 3.41 | 2.22 | 3.77 |
| New Hampshire | 1.53 | 2.60 | 1.68 | 2.86 | 1.86 | 3.17 |
| New Jersey | 19.69 | 33.48 | 21.72 | 36.93 | 24.02 | 40.84 |
| New Mexico | 2.82 | 4.80 | 3.11 | 5.29 | 3.44 | 5.85 |
| New York | 71.82 | 122.12 | 79.22 | 134.70 | 87.62 | 148.98 |
| North Carolina | 11.58 | 19.69 | 12.78 | 21.72 | 14.13 | 24.02 |
| North Dakota | 1.48 | 2.51 | 1.63 | 2.77 | 1.80 | 3.07 |
| Ohio | 23.70 | 40.29 | 26.14 | 44.44 | 28.91 | 49.15 |
| Oklahoma | 5.45 | 9.27 | 6.01 | 10.22 | 6.65 | 11.31 |
| Oregon | 6.33 | 10.77 | 6.99 | 11.88 | 7.73 | 13.14 |
| Pennsylvania | 26.53 | 45.11 | 29.26 | 49.76 | 32.37 | 55.03 |
| Rhode Island | 2.31 | 3.92 | 2.55 | 4.33 | 2.82 | 4.79 |
| South Carolina | 5.11 | 8.69 | 5.64 | 9.58 | 6.23 | 10.60 |
| South Dakota | 1.67 | 2.84 | 1.84 | 3.14 | 2.04 | 3.47 |
| Tennessee | 8.55 | 14.54 | 9.43 | 16.04 | 10.43 | 17.74 |
| Texas | 24.89 | 42.31 | 27.45 | 46.67 | 30.36 | 51.62 |
| Utah | 2.72 | 4.63 | 3.00 | 5.11 | 3.32 | 5.65 |
| Vermont | 1.13 | 1.93 | 1.25 | 2.13 | 1.38 | 2.35 |
| Virginia | 10.80 | 18.36 | 11.91 | 20.25 | 13.17 | 22.40 |
| Washington | 10.91 | 18.55 | 12.03 | 20.46 | 13.31 | 22.63 |
| West Virginia | 3.66 | 6.22 | 4.03 | 6.86 | 4.46 | 7.58 |
| Wisconsin | 12.28 | 20.87 | 13.54 | 23.02 | 14.94 | 25.46 |
| Wyoming | 1.10 | 1.87 | 1.22 | 2.07 | 1.34 | 2.29 |

## Table 4–6 (continued)

### MATURE TRUST FUND ESTIMATES BY STATE

($ billions)

SYSTEM B

**Number of Years of Growth in Covered Payroll, Various Interest Rates**

| | 6% | | 5% | | 4% | |
|---|---|---|---|---|---|---|
| | 10 | 15 | 10 | 15 | 10 | 15 |
| Alabama | 10.02 | 17.04 | 11.05 | 18.79 | 12.23 | 20.79 |
| Alaska | 2.67 | 4.55 | 2.95 | 5.01 | 3.26 | 5.55 |
| Arizona | 8.18 | 13.91 | 9.02 | 15.33 | 9.98 | 16.96 |
| Arkansas | 4.64 | 7.89 | 5.11 | 8.69 | 5.66 | 9.62 |
| California | 107.37 | 182.55 | 118.36 | 201.25 | 130.95 | 222.66 |
| Colorado | 9.73 | 16.54 | 10.73 | 18.24 | 11.87 | 20.18 |
| Connecticut | 12.47 | 21.20 | 13.75 | 23.38 | 15.21 | 25.86 |
| Delaware | 2.40 | 4.09 | 2.65 | 4.51 | 2.93 | 4.99 |
| Florida | 26.26 | 44.65 | 28.95 | 49.22 | 32.03 | 54.45 |
| Georgia | 15.02 | 25.54 | 16.56 | 28.16 | 18.32 | 31.16 |
| Hawaii | 4.22 | 7.18 | 4.66 | 7.92 | 5.15 | 8.76 |
| Idaho | 2.42 | 4.11 | 2.66 | 4.53 | 2.95 | 5.01 |
| Illinois | 46.67 | 79.36 | 51.45 | 87.49 | 56.93 | 96.79 |
| Indiana | 17.31 | 29.43 | 19.08 | 32.44 | 21.11 | 35.89 |
| Iowa | 10.39 | 17.66 | 11.45 | 19.47 | 12.67 | 21.54 |
| Kansas | 8.22 | 13.97 | 9.06 | 15.40 | 10.02 | 17.04 |
| Kentucky | 9.17 | 15.60 | 10.11 | 17.19 | 11.19 | 19.02 |
| Louisiana | 12.64 | 21.49 | 13.93 | 23.69 | 15.42 | 26.21 |
| Maine | 3.10 | 5.28 | 3.42 | 5.82 | 3.79 | 6.44 |
| Maryland | 17.20 | 29.24 | 18.96 | 32.24 | 20.98 | 35.67 |
| Massachusetts | 24.01 | 40.82 | 26.47 | 45.00 | 29.28 | 49.79 |
| Michigan | 40.91 | 69.55 | 45.10 | 76.68 | 48.89 | 84.83 |
| Minnesota | 16.67 | 28.35 | 18.38 | 31.25 | 20.34 | 34.58 |
| Mississippi | 5.91 | 10.05 | 6.52 | 11.08 | 7.21 | 12.26 |
| Missouri | 15.54 | 26.43 | 17.14 | 29.14 | 18.96 | 32.24 |
| Montana | 2.80 | 4.76 | 3.09 | 5.25 | 3.42 | 5.81 |
| Nebraska | 5.70 | 9.70 | 6.29 | 10.69 | 6.96 | 11.83 |
| Nevada | 2.69 | 4.57 | 2.96 | 5.03 | 3.28 | 5.57 |
| New Hampshire | 2.25 | 3.83 | 2.48 | 4.22 | 2.75 | 4.67 |
| New Jersey | 29.05 | 49.40 | 32.03 | 54.46 | 35.44 | 60.25 |
| New Mexico | 4.17 | 7.08 | 4.59 | 7.81 | 5.08 | 8.64 |
| New York | 105.99 | 180.21 | 116.84 | 198.67 | 129.27 | 219.80 |
| North Carolina | 17.09 | 29.06 | 18.84 | 32.04 | 20.85 | 34.45 |
| North Dakota | 2.18 | 3.71 | 2.41 | 4.09 | 2.66 | 4.53 |
| Ohio | 34.97 | 59.46 | 38.55 | 65.54 | 42.65 | 72.52 |
| Oklahoma | 8.04 | 13.68 | 8.87 | 15.08 | 9.81 | 16.68 |
| Oregon | 9.35 | 15.89 | 10.30 | 17.52 | 11.40 | 19.39 |
| Pennsylvania | 39.15 | 66.57 | 43.16 | 73.39 | 47.75 | 81.19 |
| Rhode Island | 3.41 | 5.79 | 3.75 | 6.38 | 4.15 | 7.06 |
| South Carolina | 7.54 | 12.82 | 8.31 | 14.13 | 9.20 | 15.64 |
| South Dakota | 2.47 | 4.20 | 2.72 | 4.63 | 3.01 | 5.12 |
| Tennessee | 12.62 | 21.46 | 13.91 | 23.66 | 15.39 | 26.17 |
| Texas | 36.72 | 62.44 | 40.48 | 68.83 | 44.79 | 76.16 |
| Utah | 4.02 | 6.83 | 4.43 | 7.53 | 4.90 | 8.33 |
| Vermont | 1.67 | 2.84 | 1.84 | 3.13 | 2.04 | 3.47 |
| Virginia | 15.94 | 27.09 | 17.57 | 29.87 | 19.44 | 33.05 |
| Washington | 16.10 | 27.38 | 17.75 | 30.18 | 19.64 | 33.39 |
| West Virginia | 5.39 | 9.17 | 5.95 | 10.11 | 6.58 | 11.19 |
| Wisconsin | 18.11 | 30.80 | 19.97 | 33.95 | 22.09 | 37.57 |
| Wyoming | 1.63 | 2.76 | 1.79 | 3.05 | 1.98 | 3.37 |

the assumptions of retirement at age sixty-five, ten years of payroll growth, a 6 percent interest rate and a twenty-seven-year amortization period. The highest estimated annual payments, shown in column (18), arise when retirement is at age sixty, the payroll grows for fifteen years, the interest rate is 4 percent and the amortization period is twenty-seven years. Column (25) shows the actual trust fund contributions in 1972. The actual contributions are subtracted from both the low estimate and the high estimate and presented in columns (26) and (27). These figures must be analyzed with extreme caution. They may not indicate financial irresponsibility and they may not indicate whether actual state and local retirement systems are fully funded. They do, however, provide a range of estimates of potential additional fiscal pressure on state and local governments. The striking feature of these estimates is the width of the range measured either by the difference between columns (1) and (18) or the difference between columns (26) and (27). For an interpretation of these data, the state of California can serve as an illustration.

The calculations for California show that the necessary annual payments to the trust fund over the next twenty-seven years fall somewhere between $307.9 million and $4,054.1 million. The actual 1972 payment was $636.4 million. Thus, under the most conservative assumptions the contribution was more than twice the needed amount, but according to the least conservative assumptions the contribution was $3,417.4 million short of the needed amount. This means that if California wished to have a pension system that allowed retirement at age sixty and provided pension benefits equal to the employee's average salary, and if covered payroll could be expected to increase at an annual rate of 11.2 percent for the next fifteen years, and if the interest rate were 4 percent, then in order for the unfunded balance to be eliminated by year 2000, it would be necessary for California's annual trust fund contribution to be increased to $4,054.1 million for the next twenty-seven years.

The annual payments into trust funds, however, will not be at a constant level if the most likely financing strategy is for states to extend their amortization periods periodically. Under these conditions the estimates of system B′ may provide a better indication of the required annual payments to trust fund accounts than the estimates of system B. Table 4–8 presents the system B′ estimates that would be required over the period from 1973 to 1980 with a 5 to 6 percent rate earned on trust fund assets. The annual payments rise over time since under system B′ with each passing year an additional year of payroll growth is anticipated.

**Table 4–8**

ESTIMATED REQUIRED ANNUAL PAYMENTS TO TRUST FUND ACCOUNTS, ALL STATE AND LOCAL GOVERNMENTS COMBINED, 1973–1980

($ billions)

| Year | Rate of Earnings on Trust Fund Assets | |
|---|---|---|
| | 6% | 5% |
| 1973 | 7.8 | 12.0 |
| 1974 | 8.3 | 12.8 |
| 1975 | 9.0 | 13.7 |
| 1976 | 9.7 | 14.8 |
| 1977 | 10.4 | 15.9 |
| 1978 | 11.3 | 17.2 |
| 1979 | 12.3 | 18.6 |
| 1980 | 13.4 | 20.3 |

**Source:** Table 4–4.

## Conclusions

According to the model of pension fund financing presented in this chapter, the needed annual payments to trust fund accounts for all state and local governments combined for the period from 1973 to 1980 would fall between $3.6 billion and $32.2 billion. It must be remembered that these are the amounts needed to finance the unfunded balances derived from the estimated values of the mature trust fund (*MTF*) and that it has been assumed that interest earnings on trust fund assets remain in the trust fund until the unfunded balance has been eliminated. Thus, until the needed mature trust fund (*MTF*) assets have been accumulated, the total contributions must be sufficient to cover annual pension payments and to provide the needed extra funds to build the trust fund. When the mature trust fund has been achieved, the annual contributions plus the interest earnings on the trust fund assets will provide the revenues needed to finance annual pension payments.

The range of estimated annual payments to trust fund accounts is so wide as to deserve special comment. The low estimates result when it is assumed that the retirement age is sixty-five, that covered payroll increases at an annual rate of 11.2 percent for ten years, that the interest rate is 6 percent, and that the target date for eliminating the unfunded balance is the year 2000. The high estimates result when it is assumed that the retirement age is sixty, that the covered payroll increases for fifteen years, that the interest rate is 4 percent, and that the target date is the year 2000.

Although the most likely level of annual payments to the trust fund accounts cannot be determined, it is possible to narrow the range of estimates. The typical retirement age for state and local pension plans is sixty and in recent years the rate of earnings on trust fund assets has been approximately 5 percent. Since the recent trend has been in the direction of liberalizing pension plan benefits, it would seem reasonable to expect that the normal retirement age will not be raised in the near future. It also seems reasonable, given current money market conditions and the long-run trend toward higher interest rates, to expect a 5 to 6 percent rate of return on earnings on trust fund assets to continue into the near future.

Retirement at age sixty is incorporated into the estimates of system B (see Table 4–4). Thus, with interest rates at 5 to 6 percent, the range of estimates of required annual payments to trust funds becomes $7.8 billion to $23.7 billion (that is, approximately two to six times the actual contributions in 1972).

Allowing for extended amortization, the estimates of system B′ (Table 4–8) show annual payments to the trust fund (with a 6 percent interest rate) ranging from $9.0 billion in 1975 to $13.4 billion by 1980.

Although it must be recognized that some portion of these required payments will be financed by employee contributions, the wide range of estimates that exist after selection of the most reasonable assumptions suggests a final and important conclusion. Even if the rate of interest earnings on trust fund assets remains high, the retirement age is not reduced and the value of the covered payroll increases over the next decade by no more than its historical annual rate, additional contributions to achieve full funding could come to at least double the current rate. If, however, the rate of earnings on trust fund assets falls below its current level, if pension benefits are made more generous or if the value of covered payroll increases at its historic annual rate for more than ten years, it is quite probable that retirement systems will place a severe fiscal strain on state and local governments.

## Table A–1

PAYROLL AND CASH AND SECURITY HOLDINGS OF STATE AND LOCAL GOVERNMENT RETIREMENT SYSTEMS
($ thousands)

| State | Payroll 1971 | Cash and Security Holdings 1972 |
|---|---|---|
| U.S. Total (state and local) | 71,870,850.6 | 68,760.3 |
| Alabama | 870,515.5 | 609.3 |
| Alaska | 232,291.8 | 120.7 |
| Arizona | 710,265.0 | 537.8 |
| Arkansas | 417,867.7 | 256.4 |
| California | 9,323,656.6 | 11,019.9 |
| Colorado | 844,985.1 | 740.3 |
| Connecticut | 1,082,968.7 | 797.3 |
| Delaware | 208,810.9 | 1.6 |
| Florida | 2,280,219.5 | 1,501.6 |
| Georgia | 1,304,616.5 | 968.1 |
| Hawaii | 366,848.2 | 469.3 |
| Idaho | 209,787.8 | 90.2 |
| Illinois | 4,053,225.7 | 3,185.3 |
| Indiana | 1,503,073.6 | 493.0 |
| Iowa | 902,038.5 | 542.3 |
| Kansas | 713,578.1 | 267.2 |
| Kentucky | 796,518.2 | 563.6 |
| Louisiana | 1,097,563.5 | 1,229.4 |
| Maine | 269,588.0 | 185.1 |
| Maryland | 1,493,543.7 | 1,359.8 |
| Massachusetts | 2,084,853.9 | 1,170.3 |
| Michigan | 3,552,355.1 | 2,978.6 |
| Minnesota | 1,447,932.4 | 1,066.9 |
| Mississippi | 513,271.1 | 250.5 |
| Missouri | 1,349,922.8 | 907.7 |
| Montana | 243,306.6 | 163.0 |
| Nebraska | 495,328.0 | 130.0 |
| Nevada | 233,190.6 | 176.8 |
| New Hampshire | 195,705.7 | 154.1 |
| New Jersey | 2,523,117.1 | 2,556.8 |
| New Mexico | 361,700.2 | 245.7 |
| New York | 9,204,169.1 | 14,851.3 |
| North Carolina | 1,484,263.1 | 1,389.8 |
| North Dakota | 189,519.3 | 55.7 |

Table A–1 (continued)

| State | Payroll 1971 | Cash and Security Holdings 1972 |
|---|---|---|
| Ohio | 3,032,618.5 | 4,708.6 |
| Oklahoma | 698,627.3 | 298.1 |
| Oregon | 811,755.4 | 517.1 |
| Pennsylvania | 3,399,929.1 | 3,617.3 |
| Rhode Island | 295,747.6 | 237.2 |
| South Carolina | 652,826.1 | 632.3 |
| South Dakota | 214,299.5 | 34.4 |
| Tennessee | 1,095,993.8 | 676.3 |
| Texas | 3,189,018.8 | 2,360.3 |
| Utah | 348,853.2 | 186.3 |
| Vermont | 145,226.5 | 105.3 |
| Virginia | 1,383,814.3 | 784.0 |
| Washington | 1,398,228.2 | 1,243.8 |
| West Virginia | 468,432.2 | 289.3 |
| Wisconsin | 1,573,037.2 | 1,902.5 |
| Wyoming | 141,200.4 | 70.5 |

**Source:** U.S. Bureau of the Census, *Census of Governments: Employee-Retirement Systems of State and Local Governments* (Washington, D. C.: Government Printing Office, 1974).

# 5

# PROJECTIONS OF THE STATE-LOCAL SECTOR

*David J. Ott and Attiat F. Ott*

Since the ultimate purpose of this study is to project the path of state and local government receipts and expenditures and the sector's budget surplus or deficit in the latter part of the 1970s, the general government model described in Chapter 2 and the trust fund model described in Chapter 4 were integrated with the AEI Budget and Resource Allocation Projection Model (BRAP). The BRAP model was itself changed considerably from the 1973 version, and the state and local sector's financial outlook was simulated assuming implementation of the fiscal year 1975 federal budget, with alternative assumptions on the rate of inflation and the unemployment rate. This chapter reports on the results of these simulations for the period from 1976 to 1980.

## Assumptions

The AEI model was run with three assumptions on the annual rate of inflation from 1975 to 1980 (private GNP deflator)—zero, 4, and 8 percent. In all cases, a rate of 9 percent was assumed for 1974; the "steady state" was assumed to begin in 1975 and continue thereafter. (The work here was done in the summer of 1974, before the inappropriateness of the 1974 inflation assumption was evident.) The model was run with assumptions of a 4.7 and a 4.0 percent unemployment rate. The discussion here is based on the 4.7 percent unemployment-

The authors wish to thank James J. Breen for his work in refining the AEI-BRAP model and running the simulations reported here, and to acknowledge the assistance of Debbie Ott and Bruce Henderson of Data Resources, Inc., in clearing up problems encountered in the simulation. In addition, thanks are due to Breen, Lawrence J. Korb, and Armando Baquiero for their work in projecting to 1980 parts of the 1975 federal budget totals.

rate assumption—an assumption in line with recent views as to what constitutes "full employment."[1] Since, as it turns out, the results are sensitive to the inflation assumption, state and local government budget paths are simulated for a 4 percent inflation rate and for a zero inflation rate. This is not to say that an inflation rate within this range is necessarily a reasonable prospect for the years from 1976 to 1980. However, the range does cover the inflation rates considered "acceptable" before the 1973–1974 experience.

The model assumes the fiscal year 1975 budget proposed by the Nixon administration to be in effect throughout the period.[2] At the same time, alternative inflation assumptions are allowed to affect federal receipts and expenditures (including grants to the states).

The municipal bond rate (*RM*), an important determinant of state and local construction, was held constant throughout the simulation period. Since this rate runs off the corporate bond rate, this meant setting the corporate rate at a level consistent with each specific inflation rate (the estimated "real" rate being 2.8 percent). The discount rate used to calculate state and local trust fund contributions was assumed to be the previous year's average rate of return on the assets of the trust funds. The average rate of return on state and local trust fund assets (*RSTFA*) was estimated by a regression to be a function of the Aaa corporate bond rate (*RCT*) in the previous eight years with variable weights.[3] It would thus respond only slowly to changes in the assumed market rate of interest when inflation assumptions were varied. This is consistent with the notion that actuaries, in making calculations of needed government contributions to trust funds, use earnings history rather than current market interest rates and that they will adjust with a long lag to a change in the steady-

---

[1] See, for example, the discussion by William Fellner in "Employment Goals and Monetary-Fiscal Overexpansion," in Phillip Cagan et al., *A New Look at Inflation: Economic Policy in the Early 1970s* (Washington, D. C.: American Enterprise Institute, 1973), Chapter 5, and *The Annual Report of the Council of Economic Advisers, 1974* (Washington, D. C.: Government Printing Office, February 1974), pp. 60-61.

[2] The assumptions made in projecting the federal budget to 1980 are available from the authors on request.

[3] The estimating equation was:

$$RSTFA = .00502 + \sum_{i=-1}^{-8} w_i \, RCT_i$$

| | | | |
|---|---|---|---|
| $w_{-1} = .000082$ | $w_{-5} = .001339$ | Sum of coefficients | $= .008693$ |
| $w_{-2} = .000453$ | $w_{-6} = .001182$ | Mean lag | $= 4.76$ |
| | | $\bar{R}^2$ | $= .980$ |
| $w_{-3} = .000884$ | $w_{-7} = .001040$ | *DW* | $= 1.5530$ |
| $w_{-4} = .001218$ | $w_{-8} = .001125$ | Period | $= 1955\text{-}1972$ |

state rate of interest—a lag that reflects the period it takes to turn over the asset portfolio.

The choice of the rate of growth of state and local government employment for the trust fund model posed some difficulty. While the AEI model generates the actual rate of growth of employment, the appropriate rate of growth for the trust fund calculations should be some expected rate of growth used in actuarial calculations. After we looked at the actual rate of growth of state and local government employment in the past few years, we assumed a rate of 3.5 percent to apply for the trust fund calculations throughout the period.[4] At the same time, the amortization period was set at thirty-five years, which produced a value of *An*—the excess of contributions over benefits—roughly consistent with the actual 1973 data (with the 4 percent inflation assumption).

Finally, population, public school enrollment and the labor force were projected on the basis of Census Series E data, and state and local government pension benefit payments were projected to rise, over the amortization period, to be consistent with the percent of payroll discussed in Chapter 4.

### The Simulation Results

Table 5–1 shows the path of state and local receipts, expenditures, and the surplus on an NIA basis for the years from 1976 to 1980, assuming zero and 4 percent inflation and a 4.7 percent unemployment rate. Table 5–1 shows that, with an inflation rate of 4 percent assumed, the state and local government sector runs substantial and increasing surpluses from 1976 to 1980; the overall surplus is $11.5 billion in 1976 and rises to $17.3 billion in 1980. On the other hand, if a zero inflation rate is assumed, the projected surpluses are reduced sharply at first but rise almost to the same level as with 4 percent inflation by 1980. Instead of ranging from $11.5 billion to $17.3 billion from 1976 to 1980, they range from $3.2 billion in 1976 to $15.4 billion in 1980. In 1976, for example, while both receipts and expenditures are lower for zero inflation than for 4 percent inflation, receipts fall by about $8.5 billion more than expenditures, cutting the surplus by that amount. However, in 1980, the fall in receipts is only $1.8 billion more than the fall in expenditures and the state-local

[4] The rate of growth of state and local government employment (general government) from 1963 to 1973 was 4.7 percent per annum; it was 3.3 percent a year from 1968 to 1973. However, this rate of growth slowed down after 1970, to 2.6 percent in 1973, and the slowdown is assumed to be partially perceived in the "actuarial" calculations involved.

**Table 5–1**

PROJECTED RECEIPTS, EXPENDITURES AND SURPLUS IN THE STATE AND LOCAL SECTOR, 1976–1980

(NIA basis, billions of current dollars)

| Item | 1976 | 1977 | 1978 | 1979 | 1980 |
|---|---|---|---|---|---|
| | A. Assuming 4 percent inflation and 4.7 percent unemployment rate | | | | |
| Receipts | | | | | |
| Personal tax and nontax receipts | 75.7 | 90.6 | 108.2 | 129.1 | 153.9 |
| Indirect business taxes | 119.8 | 130.9 | 142.5 | 154.8 | 167.2 |
| Corporate taxes | 9.7 | 10.6 | 11.6 | 12.6 | 13.7 |
| Contributions for social insurance | 15.3 | 17.6 | 20.6 | 24.6 | 30.0 |
| Grants | 52.3 | 55.4 | 58.6 | 61.9 | 65.5 |
| Total receipts | 272.8 | 305.1 | 341.5 | 383.0 | 430.3 |
| Expenditures | | | | | |
| Purchases | 250.7 | 280.7 | 314.3 | 351.8 | 393.8 |
| Transfers | 20.7 | 23.3 | 26.3 | 29.9 | 34.1 |
| Net interest paid | −3.4 | −4.0 | −4.6 | −5.0 | −5.7 |
| Subsidies less surplus of government enterprise | −6.6 | −7.2 | −7.8 | −8.5 | −9.2 |
| Total expenditures | 261.4 | 292.8 | 328.2 | 368.2 | 413.0 |
| Surplus or deficit (−) | 11.5 | 12.3 | 13.4 | 14.8 | 17.3 |
| | B. Assuming no inflation and 4.7 percent unemployment rate | | | | |
| Receipts | | | | | |
| Personal tax and nontax receipts | 69.7 | 80.2 | 92.3 | 106.0 | 121.7 |
| Indirect business taxes | 109.2 | 108.3 | 107.0 | 104.1 | 99.4 |
| Corporate taxes | 8.9 | 9.4 | 9.9 | 10.3 | 10.8 |
| Contributions for social insurance | 13.6 | 16.5 | 20.4 | 25.3 | 31.6 |
| Grants | 49.6 | 50.8 | 51.9 | 53.1 | 54.4 |
| Total receipts | 251.0 | 265.2 | 281.5 | 298.8 | 317.9 |
| Expenditures | | | | | |
| Purchases | 236.0 | 247.1 | 259.0 | 271.0 | 283.4 |
| Transfers | 19.7 | 21.1 | 22.7 | 24.6 | 26.7 |
| Net interest paid | −1.6 | −1.3 | −1.0 | −0.6 | −0.3 |
| Subsidies less surplus of government enterprise | −6.1 | −6.4 | −6.7 | −0.7 | −7.3 |
| Total expenditures | 248.0 | 260.5 | 274.0 | 288.0 | 302.5 |
| Surplus or deficit (−) | 3.2 | 4.7 | 7.4 | 10.8 | 15.4 |

**Note:** Details may not add to totals because of rounding.
**Source:** BRAP estimates.

budget surplus is only $1.8 billion below its level at the 4 percent inflation rate. The model suggests in the short run, as with the federal budget,[5] inflation affects receipts more than expenditures; a higher inflation rate thus generates larger nominal full employment surpluses for the state-local sector. The explanation for the diverse short-run/long-run behavior of the surplus as inflation rates differ is discussed below.

If one assumes that the inflation rate from 1975 to 1980 will be somewhere in the range from zero to 4 percent, the state and local government sector will, according to the projections made here, show an overall surplus ranging from about $3 billion to about $11 billion in 1976, which will rise to something between about $15 billion and about $17 billion by 1980.

To ascertain exactly how the inflation rate works through the state and local government model to affect the sector's full-employment surplus in the short and long run, it is necessary to look separately at the general government account and the trust funds.

**The General Government Account.** Projected receipts, expenditures and the surplus or deficit for the state and local general government account are shown, for the two inflation assumptions and for 4.7 percent unemployment, in Table 5–2. Over the period from 1976 to 1980 the general government account runs a small surplus of about $1.5 billion with the 4 percent inflation assumption; but if no inflation is assumed, the balance on general government account turns into a deficit, which begins at $4.1 billion in 1976 and decreases to $2.2 billion by 1980. The difference in the overall state and local government sector's budget position under the two inflation assumptions is thus largely explained by the turnaround in the general government budget balance, and the general government account explains more of the difference as the years pass after 1976. In 1976, the general government account explains $5.5 billion of the $8.3 billion difference in the overall state and local budget surplus with the two inflation assumptions. By 1980 it more than explains the difference—while the combined budget surplus is $1.8 billion higher with 4 percent inflation, the turnaround on the general government account is $3.8 billion.

A close look at the expenditure section of Table 5–2 makes it clear that the major force which keeps expenditures from rising as much as receipts is construction outlays. This in turn reflects the impact of interest rates on education and "other" real construction in the general government model (Chapter 2). A higher "steady state"

[5] See *Annual Report of the Council of Economic Advisers, 1974*, esp. pp. 79-80.

## Table 5–2

PROJECTED RECEIPTS, EXPENDITURES AND SURPLUS, STATE AND LOCAL GENERAL GOVERNMENT SECTOR, 1976–1980

(NIA basis, billions of current dollars)

| Item | 1976 | 1977 | 1978 | 1979 | 1980 |
|---|---|---|---|---|---|
| | A. Assuming 4 percent inflation and 4.7 percent unemployment rate | | | | |
| Receipts | | | | | |
| Personal tax and nontax receipts | 75.7 | 90.6 | 108.2 | 129.1 | 153.9 |
| Indirect business taxes | 119.8 | 130.9 | 142.5 | 154.8 | 167.2 |
| Corporate taxes | 9.7 | 10.6 | 11.6 | 12.6 | 13.7 |
| Grants | 52.3 | 55.4 | 58.6 | 61.9 | 65.5 |
| Total receipts | 257.6 | 287.5 | 320.9 | 358.4 | 400.3 |
| Expenditures | | | | | |
| Current account purchases | 215.3 | 243.0 | 274.0 | 308.8 | 347.8 |
| Construction | 35.4 | 37.7 | 40.3 | 43.0 | 46.0 |
| Transfer payments (except trust funds) | 8.6 | 8.8 | 9.1 | 9.4 | 9.8 |
| Interest paid | 3.5 | 3.7 | 3.9 | 4.1 | 4.3 |
| Subsidies less surplus of government enterprise | −6.6 | −7.2 | −7.8 | −8.5 | −9.2 |
| Total expenditures | 256.2 | 286.0 | 319.4 | 356.8 | 398.7 |
| Surplus or deficit (−) | 1.4 | 1.5 | 1.5 | 1.6 | 1.6 |
| | B. Assuming no inflation and 4.7 percent unemployment rate | | | | |
| Receipts | | | | | |
| Personal tax and nontax receipts | 69.7 | 80.2 | 92.3 | 106.0 | 121.7 |
| Indirect business taxes | 109.2 | 108.3 | 107.0 | 104.1 | 99.4 |
| Corporate taxes | 8.9 | 9.4 | 9.9 | 10.3 | 10.8 |
| Grants | 49.6 | 50.8 | 51.9 | 53.1 | 54.4 |
| Total receipts | 237.5 | 248.7 | 261.1 | 273.5 | 286.3 |
| Expenditures | | | | | |
| Current account purchases | 194.3 | 204.8 | 215.9 | 227.1 | 238.6 |
| Construction | 41.7 | 42.3 | 43.0 | 43.8 | 44.7 |
| Transfer payments (except trust funds) | 8.0 | 7.9 | 7.9 | 7.9 | 7.9 |
| Subsidies less surplus of government enterprise | −6.1 | −6.4 | −6.7 | −7.0 | −7.3 |
| Total expenditures | 241.6 | 252.5 | 264.3 | 276.2 | 288.5 |
| Surplus or deficit (−) | −4.1 | −3.8 | −3.2 | −2.7 | −2.2 |

**Note:** Details may not add to totals because of rounding.

**Source:** BRAP estimates.

inflation rate produces a higher nominal municipal bond rate and a lower "steady state" path for real construction outlays. The higher cost of construction which accompanies the higher rate of inflation is not enough to keep current dollar construction outlays from falling—in 1976 current dollars outlays for construction would be about $42 billion if zero inflation is assumed; the assumption of 4 percent inflation a year and the attendant higher interest rate causes these 1976 outlays to drop to around $35 billion. This alone would more than account for the switch from a deficit to a surplus when the 4 percent inflation rate replaces the zero inflation rate.

It accounts also for the downward drift of the deficit when zero percent inflation is assumed, a pattern which does not appear if 4 percent inflation is assumed. With a zero inflation rate and thus a lower interest rate, real construction expenditures are higher in 1976 than with 4 percent inflation and a higher interest rate. (In 1958 prices, construction outlays in 1976 are 29 percent higher with zero inflation than with 4 percent inflation.) However, given this permanent effect of the lower interest rate on real outlays, the gap between current dollar outlays narrows as time passes. With 4 percent inflation (and the lower real path of construction outlays), nominal construction outlays grow faster than with the alternative inflation assumption because of the more rapid rise in the price indices for state and local government construction.

As noted in Chapter 1, the general government account showed persistent and generally increasing deficits through 1969 when it ran a deficit of $5 billion. Its deficit then grew smaller and turned into a surplus of $4 billion in 1972, and in 1973 the general government budget was virtually in balance. The projections in Table 5–2 suggest that the 1969–1973 turnaround in the general government account may not be purely a temporary phenomenon; the range of projected general government surpluses shown there suggests that fiscal pressures on the state and local government may be less, by this measure, than in the 1950s and 1960s. Instead of $5 billion or $6 billion deficits, the general government account, depending on the rate of inflation, may run closer to a balanced budget or even show small surpluses at full employment in the last part of the 1970s. Whatever the inflation assumption and the resulting surplus or deficit, the difference between these projections and the figures for the 1950s and 1960s is that the balance in general government account should tend to improve (or at worst not deteriorate) from 1976 on under full employment conditions, rather than showing a trend toward larger and larger deficits as it did in the 1950s and 1960s.

The major force producing the switch from the pattern of increasing deficits in the 1950s and 1960s is a projected slowdown in real state and local government construction outlays. Such outlays grew at a rate of about 5 percent per annum from 1953 to 1969, and at a rate of 4.5 percent per annum from 1961 to 1969. The general government model shows virtually no real growth in construction outlays from 1976 to 1980 with either inflation assumption; growth in the nominal amount of such outlays depends mostly on the rate of inflation. (Since construction costs ordinarily outrun the general rate of inflation, nominal outlays grow even when the overall inflation rate is zero.) Real outlays for all categories of construction—education, highways, and "other"—are projected to grow at much slower rates than in the 1950s or 1960s, and real highway construction declines from 1976 to 1980. This decline is just slightly more than offset by a growth of 11 percent in real "other" construction. Real education construction is flat over the period, contrasted to a growth rate of 4.4 percent a year from 1961 to 1969.[6]

At the same time that constant dollar construction outlays are growing slowly, constant dollar construction grants are growing rapidly—16 percent from 1976 to 1980—largely because of rapid growth in pollution control grants by the Environmental Protection Agency and grants for mass transit. Since these newer grant programs have higher federal matching rates than the previous mix of non-highway grants, they mandate less state-local construction per dollar of grants. The growth of grants thus outstrips the growth of construction outlays, and the general government deficit is reduced or turned into a small surplus.

**The Trust Funds.** The inflation assumption also affects the projected surplus in the trust funds, as Table 5–3 shows. However, the direction of the effect is different in the short run from what it is in the long run. In the short run, a higher rate of inflation causes both receipts (contributions for social insurance along with investment income) and expenditures (benefit payments) [7] to rise, but receipts to rise more than expenditures. The reason for this lies in the way the trust fund model calculates *An*—the excess of contributions over benefits—and the way benefits are calculated. *An* is calculated by projection of

[6] Real highway construction declines with completion of the interstate system and a slower rate of growth in highway grants than in the past. The minimal growth in school construction reflects an absolute decline in student enrollment from 1975 to 1980 (based on Census Series E-2 projections of enrollment).

[7] Expenditures of the trust funds also include administrative expenses, but these are so small they were ignored in the long-run expenditure projections.

### Table 5–3

PROJECTED RECEIPTS, EXPENDITURES AND SURPLUS, STATE AND LOCAL TRUST FUNDS, 1976–1980

(NIA basis, billions of current dollars)

| Item | 1976 | 1977 | 1978 | 1979 | 1980 |
|---|---|---|---|---|---|
| | A. Assuming 4 percent inflation and 4.7 percent unemployment rate | | | | |
| Receipts | | | | | |
| Contributions for social insurance | 15.3 | 17.6 | 20.6 | 24.6 | 30.1 |
| Investment income | 7.0 | 7.7 | 8.4 | 9.1 | 9.9 |
| Total receipts | 22.3 | 25.3 | 29.1 | 33.7 | 40.0 |
| Expenditures | | | | | |
| Benefit payments | 12.2 | 14.5 | 17.2 | 20.4 | 24.3 |
| Total expenditures | 12.2 | 14.5 | 17.2 | 20.4 | 24.3 |
| Surplus or deficit (−) | 10.1 | 10.8 | 11.8 | 13.3 | 15.7 |
| | B. Assuming no inflation and 4.7 percent unemployment rate | | | | |
| Receipts | | | | | |
| Contributions for social insurance | 13.6 | 16.5 | 20.4 | 25.3 | 31.6 |
| Investment income | 5.3 | 5.3 | 5.1 | 4.9 | 4.8 |
| Total receipts | 18.9 | 21.7 | 25.4 | 30.2 | 36.5 |
| Expenditures | | | | | |
| Benefit payments | 11.7 | 13.2 | 14.8 | 16.7 | 18.9 |
| Total expenditures | 11.7 | 13.2 | 14.8 | 16.7 | 18.9 |
| Surplus or deficit (−) | 7.3 | 8.5 | 10.6 | 13.5 | 17.6 |

**Note:** Details may not add to totals because of rounding.
**Source:** BRAP estimates.

benefits and contributions, taking the present value of each, and amortizing the unfunded liability (the difference between the present value of benefits and contributions and the accumulated trust fund in the future). In the projection of benefits and contributions, the key variables are the rate of growth of the state and local payroll (in current dollars) and the discount rate. Payroll is assumed to grow at a rate equal to the sum of the rate of growth of employment (3.5 percent a year, as noted above), the rate of growth of productivity (assumed constant at 3 percent), and the rate of inflation. Given the discount rate, a higher rate of inflation raises the present value of contributions and benefits and thus the value of the mature trust fund (*MTF*), all in the same proportion. And, given the discount rate, the accumulated trust fund would grow to the same level regardless of the rate of inflation. Therefore, the unfunded liability (*UB*) to be amortized and paid in as contributions over and above current pensions (as *An*) increases by a greater proportion than the present value of future benefits, future contributions and the *MTF*. Hence, since receipts are calculated as contributions (*An* and current benefits) plus investment income, they rise more than current benefits rise, and, in the short run, the trust fund surplus grows larger.

Obviously, what this outline does not capture is the fact that the discount rate will not remain constant if the rate of inflation varies between zero and 4 percent. In most state and local government pension plans, the discount rate is roughly related to the average rate of return on pension fund assets in the recent past (six to ten years). As noted earlier, the model here estimates the discount rate (the average rate of return on trust fund assets) as a function of the corporate bond rate lagged eight years (with variable weights). Thus, if the rate of inflation is assumed to rise from zero to 4 percent a year over time, the average rate of return on the assets of pension funds shows an upward trend. And the effect of a higher discount rate is to sharply decrease the value of *An*—the excess of (employer and employee) contributions over current pension benefits required to fund future benefits. This occurs because trust fund assets grow more rapidly the greater the investment income from the higher interest (discount) rate, and because a higher discount rate reduces the annual amount needed to amortize the (larger) unfunded liability.

As shown in Table 5–3, a higher rate of inflation produces a larger state and local government sector trust fund surplus in the short run than does zero inflation. This result reflects the short-run effect of higher inflation and a larger unfunded liability. But in the long run, a higher rate of inflation produces a smaller surplus as the discount rate used in computing *An* gradually adjusts to the higher market rate of interest. Thus, the trust fund surplus for 4 percent inflation falls below that for zero inflation by 1979, and this shortfall widens in 1980. In brief, while a higher rate of inflation works to increase the immediate surplus (reduce the immediate deficit) on the general government account, in the longer run it tends to reduce the surplus in the trust funds. This is the reason the overall state and local government surplus shown in Table 5–1 is not widely different for either inflation assumption by 1980, while there is a sharp difference in the short run. In general, with both the current account and the trust funds being considered, a high rate of inflation produces a large surplus in the short run, while in the long run, although the surplus is still there, it is not as large.[8]

---

[8] When an inflation rate of 8 percent was assumed, the overall surplus of the state and local government sector was $22 billion in 1980.

Thus, the outlook for the overall state and local government surplus is subject to considerable uncertainty in the near term because of uncertainty about the rate of inflation and the 1974–1975 recession. In the longer run, however, the projections here suggest a continual tendency for large and growing surpluses by this sector (given the long-run inflation and discount rate assumptions). This outlook is clouded by the basic and somewhat tenuous assumption underlying the trust fund projection—that there is a continuation of the degree of funding of these plans consistent with the model discussed in Chapter 4. However, as was noted in Chapter 3, the degree of funding in the major state and local plans varies widely. There is no assurance that the average degree of funding prevailing in 1972 will hold for the future. Two crosscurrents are at work: (1) many larger state and local plans have moved to improve the funding of their plans and to require periodic actuarial review of their funding status; but (2) on the other hand, there is a natural tendency for state and local politicians to take a short-term view (corresponding to their term of office) and to thus defer increased government contributions if it means raising taxes. There is no scientific way to determine which pressure will prevail; allowance must be made for this uncertainty in using the surpluses projected here for the trust funds.

**The Outlook for State and Local Taxes.** Projections under plausible assumptions of the surpluses (or deficits) which the state and local government sector may run are important for the shaping of federal fiscal policy. To the extent that the state and local government sector shows a larger surplus (smaller deficit) at full employment (given the desired level of aggregate demand), the federal budget can be shaped to show less restraint (a smaller full-employment surplus or a larger deficit on a full-employment basis).[9]

However, from the standpoint of state and local government officials and particularly from the standpoint of the taxpayer, a more immediate issue is the outlook for state and local tax burdens. Given the projected state and local government budget outlook, it may be asked what is implied about the "fiscal pressure on the state and their local entities." Will there be a pattern of continued tax rate increases (as distinguished from revenue growth through increases in the tax base) as there was in the 1950s and 1960s, or will there not?

The general government model was constructed, as noted in Chapter 2, with this question in mind. Rather than attempting to

[9] This was discussed at some length in David J. Ott et al., *Public Claims on U.S. Output*, and in *Report of the Council of Economic Advisers, 1974.*

estimate paths for each of the various state and local taxes, it was assumed that (1) state and local general government tax revenue (*STAXGG*) would be "pulled" along by expenditures; *STAXGG* was assumed to be equal to total general government outlays less federal grants with the surplus on general government account added in. Put another way, total general government tax revenue was assumed to be sufficient to balance current account expenditures along with the portion of construction outlays financed by tax revenues (*TAXI*).

To get some idea of the implications of the model's projections for tax rate increases (or decreases), as opposed to growth in revenues from growth in the tax base (resulting in turn from growth in the economy), it was arbitrarily assumed that state corporate taxes and personal income taxes would grow at a rate consistent with no rate increases. Corporate tax revenues were assumed to grow proportionately with corporate profits, and personal taxes were assumed to grow by 1.1 percent for each 1 percent growth in taxable personal income. Thus, since personal and corporate taxes are assumed not to reflect rate increases, the behavior of state and local indirect business taxes (*SIBT*)—including both property taxes and sales-excise taxes—could be monitored to ascertain, at least roughly, to what extent rate increases would be implied by the need to raise the revenues implied by the expenditure path. As a criterion, we used a comparison of the rates of growth of state and local indirect business taxes and current-dollar GNP. It was plausible to assume that the base for both taxes—property and sales—would grow roughly with the value of total output. If *SIBT* grew no faster or slower than GNP, it might be inferred that there would be no rate increases, or that there even might be cuts in rates. On the other hand, if *SIBT* grew faster than GNP, then the state-local budget projections might be assumed to reflect a need for further tax rate increases in the period from 1976 to 1980.

Table 5–4 compares the annual rates of growth of GNP and *SIBT* for the zero and 4 percent inflation assumptions. With the assumption of 4 percent inflation, the rate of growth of state and local indirect business taxes would be slightly higher than the rate assumption of 4 percent inflation, the rate of growth of state and of growth of GNP in 1977, about the same in 1978, and thereafter less. If a zero rate of inflation were assumed, then *SIBT* actually declined over the period from 1976 to 1980, while GNP rose at a rate above 4 percent.

At least on the basis of this crude analysis, it appears that the history of sharp upward pressure on tax rates at the state and local

## Table 5–4

PROJECTED STATE-LOCAL INDIRECT BUSINESS TAXES AND GROSS NATIONAL PRODUCT, 1976–1980

(NIA basis, billions of current dollars)

| Item | 1976 | 1977 | 1978 | 1979 | 1980 |
|---|---|---|---|---|---|
| | A. Assuming 4 percent inflation and 4.7 percent unemployment | | | | |
| State-local indirect business taxes (*SIBT*) | 119.8 | 130.9 | 142.5 | 154.8 | 167.2 |
| Gross national product (GNP) | 1,743.0 | 1,896.0 | 2,062.6 | 2,239.0 | 2,428.0 |
| Annual rate of change of *SIBT* (percent) | — | 9.3 | 8.9 | 8.6 | 8.0 |
| Annual rate of change of GNP (percent) | — | 8.8 | 8.8 | 8.6 | 8.4 |
| | B. Assuming no inflation and 4.7 percent unemployment | | | | |
| State-local indirect business taxes (*SIBT*) | 109.2 | 108.3 | 107.0 | 104.1 | 99.4 |
| Gross national product (GNP) | 1,607.0 | 1,683.0 | 1,761.0 | 1,840.0 | 1,921.0 |
| Annual rate of change of *SIBT* (percent) | — | −0.8 | −1.2 | −2.7 | −4.5 |
| Annual rate of change of GNP (percent) | — | 4.7 | 4.6 | 4.5 | 4.4 |

**Source:** BRAP estimates.

level, such as experienced in the 1950s and 1960s, is not likely to continue into the last part of the 1970s. Indeed, it is possible, depending on the inflation rate, to envisage at least some cuts in state and local tax rates.

However, this calculation ignores an important point obscured when the NIA breakdown between the general government account and the trust funds is used. State and local governments must also raise taxes to finance the government share of contributions to the trust funds. In recent years, the employer's (governmental) share of state and local government contributions for social insurance have grown much more rapidly than the employee's share, and, more important, the employer's share has been rising as a percent of payroll —from about 7.7 percent of wages and salaries in 1969 to 8.1 percent in 1973.[10] Thus, to reflect the pressures on state and local tax rates, the government share of state-local contributions for social insurance

[10] U.S. Department of Commerce, *Survey of Current Business*, July 1973 and July 1974, Tables 3-7 and 6-2.

(*ESCSI*) should be added to the indirect business taxes (*SIBT*) in the comparison shown in Table 5–4.

This is done in Table 5–5. Employee contributions for social insurance were assumed to grow with state and local payrolls from 1973 to 1976, and the governmental share was assumed to be the residual.

Table 5–5 casts some doubt on the previous conclusion that state and local governments will not need tax rate increases in the latter part of the 1970s. With 4 percent inflation, the required rate of increase in (*SIBT* + *ESCSI*) is greater than the rate of increase in

**Table 5–5**

PROJECTED STATE-LOCAL INDIRECT BUSINESS TAXES PLUS INDIRECT BUSINESS TAXES AND GROSS NATIONAL PRODUCT, 1976–1980

(NIA basis, billions of current dollars)

| Item | 1976 | 1977 | 1978 | 1979 | 1980 |
|---|---|---|---|---|---|
| | A. Assuming 4 percent inflation and 4.7 percent unemployment | | | | |
| State-local indirect business taxes (*SIBT*) plus employer share of contributions (*ESCSI*) | 127.1 | 140.6 | 154.2 | 169.4 | 186.9 |
| Gross national product (GNP) | 1,743.0 | 1,896.0 | 2,062.0 | 2,239.0 | 2,428.0 |
| Annual rate of change of *SIBT* and *ESCSI* (percent) | — | 10.6 | 9.7 | 9.8 | 10.3 |
| Annual rate of change of GNP (percent) | — | 8.8 | 8.8 | 8.6 | 8.4 |
| | B. Assuming no inflation and 4.7 percent unemployment | | | | |
| State-local indirect business taxes (*SIBT*) plus employer share of contributions (*ESCSI*) | 116.1 | 117.6 | 119.7 | 121.2 | 122.2 |
| Gross national product (GNP) | 1,607.0 | 1,683.0 | 1,761.0 | 1,840.0 | 1,921.0 |
| Annual rate of change of *SIBT* and *ESCSI* (percent) | — | 0.7 | 1.8 | 1.2 | 0.7 |
| Annual rate of change of GNP (percent) | — | 4.7 | 4.6 | 4.5 | 4.4 |

**Source:** BRAP estimates.

GNP. On the other hand, (*SIBT* + *ESCSI*) grows much more slowly than GNP when zero inflation is assumed.

In summary, the outlook is unclear for state and local tax rates in the years immediately ahead. The outlook is bright if the trust funds are ignored, but when the taxes needed to finance the required governmental contribution to the trust funds are included, it appears that rate increases may be required, depending on the rate of inflation. However, the pressures to finance current account and construction expenditures except governmental contributions to the trust funds seems certain to be less than in the 1950s and the 1960s.

## Conclusions

The simulation results presented in this chapter suggest that there will be a continuation of the large and growing surpluses in the state and local government sector of the NIA account. On general government account, state and local governments will experience much slower rates of real growth in expenditures in the period from 1976 to 1980 than in the 1950s and 1960s. In particular, real construction outlays seem likely to grow slowly over this period. When this is coupled with a more rapid growth in real grants for construction, it may be concluded that (depending on the rate of inflation) the general government balance should show smaller deficits than in the 1950s and 1960s (or even surpluses), and the past tendency toward larger and larger deficits should not reappear during this period.

The projections for the trust funds also suggest the likelihood of large and growing surpluses. While these surpluses are sensitive to the inflation assumption in the short run (a higher inflation rate increases the trust fund surplus), in the long run they are less sensitive and large surpluses ($15-$22 billion) are produced even with inflation rates of zero to 8 percent.

While the real world will not correspond, year in and year out, to the "steady state" explored here, the potential for larger surpluses in the state and local government sector is both a blessing and a problem. On the bright side, these surpluses will provide savings to help meet the unusually large demand for investment in the energy and pollution control areas that some envision over the next decade. On the other hand, the very size of the surpluses, and the potential short-run fluctuations they may exhibit as inflation rates and unemployment rates vary, will pose additional problems for monetary and fiscal policy makers. No longer can we ignore the state and local government sector in attempting to strike the desired balance between aggregate demand and supply.